DO-ABLE PRAYER

Seeing God's Reflection on Earth

Simple, easy, effective methods for
bringing prayer into your everyday life

Ginny Kisling

Do-Able Prayer – Additional copies can be ordered
at https://www.createspace.com/3781510

Copyright © 2012 by Virginia (Ginny) Kisling

Printed in the United States of America

ginny@harvestprayer.com
gkisling@pacbell.net

SERMON OUTLINES
Sermon outlines will be available for all the chapters. They are free and are being developed by a group of pastors. As they become available they will be uploaded and available at: http://sermons.logos.com/profile/ginny-kisling

Also to reach the sermon outlines you can Google "Ginny Kisling's Sermons & Illustrations." Once you have reached my profile you will see the names of the chapters and the chapter numbers and can select the one(s) you are seeking.

STUDY GUIDE
This book contains a built-in optional study guide at the back of each chapter that can be used either by the reader alone or within a group context.

ISBN-13: 978-1475156775
ISBN-10: 1475156774
ISBN information is registered with BooksInPrint.com®

Scripture Quotations
Any bold highlighting, italics, or underlining of Scriptures, are emphasis added by the author of this book.

All scripture quotations, unless otherwise indicated, are taken from the Holy Bible, New International Version®, NIV®. Copyright ©1973, 1978, 1984, 2011 by Biblica, Inc.™ Used by permission of Zondervan. All rights reserved worldwide. www.zondervan.com

The "NIV" and "New International Version" are trademarks registered in the United States Patent and Trademark Office by Biblica, Inc.™

Book cover and layout by Jeff Baham (www.jeffbaham.com)
Cover photo by Caitlin Childs

Table of Contents

Part One: How We Are Wired

Part Two: Do-Able Prayers For Your Sphere of Influence

Acknowledgements

From my experience in authoring a book, I can say without reservation that it just about takes a village to write one! No surprise though, this is simply an example of a truth spoken long ago by apostle Peter, "Each one should use whatever gift he has received to serve others, faithfully administering God's grace in its various forms" (1 Peter 4:10).

When we are part of God's family, we do our best work "in community." I have many words of appreciation for my *village of supporters* who also long to see prayer become *do-able* for every Christian, not just the passionate few.

First and foremost I am grateful to my parents, Marge and Sam Leach, who leave a legacy of putting God first in the home and teaching me to pray. Acknowledgements also to all my siblings, Carol, Jim, Rick and Mary, who are all part of shaping who I am today, and to my spiritual mom, Linda Beardsley, whose persistence and unconditional love drew me into a life-long love relationship with our Lord. My son Jordan deserves special thanks for taking up more than his share of keeping the home fires burning while I worked from early dawn till late evening over the duration of writing *Do-Able Prayer*.

I am grateful for the constant prayer support and words of encouragement from my up-close and personal team and treasured friends: Gini Davi, Marlene Love and Marty Van Drielen and for my prayer team at large that support me in prayer on a regular basis.

A special thanks to Susan Sagun for her skilled editing, thoughtful feedback and special friendship during the early formation of the manuscript. She continued to provide insightful feedback throughout the book writing process. Our many conversations during our walks to Starbucks kept me encouraged and refreshed!

I do not know where I would be without the expertise of a very

Godly woman and friend, Sandy Petersen, who brought an amazing gift to this project with her deep editing knowledge, intercessory calling and always knowing just want I meant to say! The words that roll over in my mind when I think of Sandy are inspired from the book of Esther. God sent her my way "...for such a time as this." Thank you, Sandy!

I want to acknowledge another group of folks who have walked with me during many of my prayer leadership years (and experiments) and have offered support, friendship and encouragement for the journey: Fran and Bill Goodrich, Milan Telian, Marina Rogers, Pastor Tim Ruiz, Paula Leonardi, Judy Adamson, Carole Swan, Doug and Sharon Lamb, Tim and Cathy Skover, Dave and Donna Lindberg and Vivian Williams.

Thanks to others who have gone before me and inspired me by standing the test of time as they faithfully served God in their ministries without fanfare or applause: Reverend Karl and Ruth Ann Overbeek, Reverend Tim Vink, Reverend John Isaacs, Reverend Susan Bagley, Dave and Kim Butts, Jon Graf, Nancy Harden and Sandra Higley.

My heart is full of gratitude for my pastor, Dwight M. Bailey Jr., a humble man of God and prayer and a constant encourager, and for Church of the Chimes, my church in San Jose, CA, under whose guidance and protection I grew in my Prayer Ministry leadership role.

I also want to acknowledge with gratitude Dr. David Cannistraci who saw God's timing for this book and encouraged me to write it. Over the years many people have prodded me to write a book, but this was the first time that the *urging* coincided with a *stirring* from God in my spirit to do so. In addition to pastoring a growing congregation, Dr. Cannistraci has given of himself sacrificially in his service and leadership to the San Francisco Bay Area and beyond in training, encouragement, and mentorship with leaders and pastors.

Many thanks to a special group of pastors who have collaborated with me in some way: Dwight Bailey Jr., Dr. David Cannistraci, Tim Vink, Scott Abke, and Dr. Samuel Nandakumar.

Last but not least my heartfelt gratitude extends to Jeff Baham, an extremely creative and talented artist who designed the book cover which truly captures the essence of this book and magnifies the Lord. Thank you, Jeff, for all your suggestions, layout work, and filling in many gaps of knowledge for me in this exciting publishing project!

Introduction

One day while meeting with a highly respected pastor in our community, we began discussing the topic of prayer. In our discussions I had referred to *Do-Able Prayer* a number of times. At the end of our meeting I asked the pastor if there was anything I could do for him. He said, "Yes! Write on *Do-able Prayer* for me. Then I would like to collaborate with you to develop some sermon outlines for my network of pastors to use, much like what noted pastor and author Bill Hybels does."

I'm always stoked about finding ways to equip and mobilize the body of Christ for prayer, but to see this pastor's enthusiasm and serious interest just added fuel to the fire for me. It was another confirmation of a strong stirring in my spirit that I already had with regard to putting pen to paper to capture what I had been discovering and speaking about over the last sixteen years. It had become evident to me in my work in the prayer ministry that prayer was not something everyone felt comfortable with, even though there was a common agreement that it was important. So it was with great joy that I undertook this project to write on a subject near and dear to my heart - *Do-Able Prayer*. In fact, it is like a dream come true!

In one way or another I have been working in the Prayer Ministry for the last sixteen years. Because of my work and affection for prayer, most people credit me with being what is termed a *Prayer Warrior*. The truth is, like many other Christians I sometimes find prayer to be a struggle. My own experience in this arena could at times be likened to one who is lugging a boulder into God's Throne Room. Yet being called to work in the prayer ministry has, over the years, enabled me to build the muscles of discipline for prayer, and I am certainly the better for it.

Early in my Christian life I discovered how to pray in private, and that is the way I liked it – private. I saw God answer my prayers in some powerful ways that, at the time, seemed almost too easy to me. In the beginning, my prayers were pretty much centered on my concerns or the needs of those with whom I was most closely connected. As I matured in my faith, the focus of my prayers began to broaden and I found myself also praying for the church and the spiritual well-being of others. There was no particular rhyme, reason, or plan to this and, in retrospect, I realize that I simply did not understand the basis for prayer, how it really worked, and why, or even if my prayers were truly necessary or made any difference.

One particular week about sixteen years ago, I felt a kind of pressing in my spirit, a sense of heightened concern for our pastor and his family. It was a difficult time for him both personally and with the church. His son Nathan needed a life-saving transplant, and our church was going through some growing pains. I called a couple from my Sunday school class and asked if they would like to join with me to pray for our pastor the following Sunday. Fran and Bill said "Yes" as they, too, were sensing that our pastor and his family could use some focused prayer. That next Sunday Fran, Bill, and I met in our usual room where it was my intention to encourage the others from our class to go hear the visiting missionary next door. To my surprise, they all wanted to stay and pray. I was momentarily speechless as I had never led a *prayer-anything* before, and now I had a dozen or so people looking to me to lead this prayer time. I stumbled through with each of us praying around the table for our dear pastor, and was relieved when the time was up!

That week I continued to feel that same pressing in my spirit, so I called Fran and Bill and asked if they would meet with me in the pastor's office to again pray for him during the Sunday school hour. They were happy to join me and that "pressing" has never since left me. Shortly thereafter I somehow acquired the title of Prayer Leader in my church, which I assure you was not anything I had earned or set out to do. It happened more by default than by design, or at least that is how it seemed to me at the time.

Thus began an amazing journey into the world of prayer and

prayer leadership. Little could I have known then where this journey would take me and how it would evolve over sixteen years' time. One thing I discovered early on is that prayer is not so *do-able* for many people. I have had a growing conviction ever since that God desires and longs for prayer to be one of the most *do-able* parts of our spiritual journey; hence, the birth of this book on *Do-Able Prayer*.

Update

The pastor's son, Nathan, received his life-saving organ transplant and he and his wife are doing well. Recently they were in town for a visit and we chatted and happily reminisced about that time sixteen years ago when everything looked so uncertain for Nathan and how God gave him an amazing miracle of life.

In reflecting upon this story about Nathan and the time of my fledgling beginnings in the prayer ministry, I was reminded of some long forgotten words spoken to me by Nathan's mother, Ruth Ann Overbeek. She and I had first met under the ministry of her husband, Karl, many years earlier in Carmichael, CA, where I had given my life in service to the Lord as a very young adult. Then, many years later she and her husband would take the pastorate of the same church I would become part of when moving to the Bay Area. One year Ruth Ann gave me a special birthday memento. Small enough to fit into the palm of my hand, it was a replica of a typewriter. It was hinged to open and revealed a small hand written note from Ruth Ann tucked inside. As she gave me the gift, she said, "I always remember your creative writing from our days in Carmichael and want to encourage you to keep writing. I see a book in your future!" I tucked it away and never gave it another thought until this moment in time.

Ruth Ann's prediction, or some might refer to it as a prophetic word, indeed came to pass with this book. "A word aptly spoken is like apples of gold in settings of silver" (Proverbs 25:11). Her timely words spoke untold blessings into my future. This book is definitely one of the fruits of Ruth Ann's and Karl's ministry labors.

My prayers and blessings go with each and every one of you as you journey with me through *Do-Able Prayer*

— **Ginny Kisling**

Foreword

I f you are a pastor, church prayer leader, or the every-day Christian ..... you are going to like this book! More than that, you are going to be helped in your prayer life by reading it. Our Harvest Prayer Ministries colleague and friend, Ginny Kisling has done us all a favor by putting together some wonderfully practical teaching and exercises in *Do-Able Prayer*.

She begins by helping unravel the confusion created by the reality of what she calls the 5% and the 95%. The lack of awareness in the church over the existence, and then the role of the intercessor have caused so many problems. *Do-Able Prayer* will help clear up a lot of misunderstanding in congregations. It might also help you as an individual handle where you are personally in your prayer life with more grace and insight.

The lack of awareness in the church over the existence, and then the role of the inter-cessor has caused so many problems. Do-Able Prayer *will help clear up a lot of misunderstanding in congregations.*

The main part of this practical handbook on prayer covers most of the major areas that are impacted by prayer including personal, family, church and nations. Of course, there are whole books written on any one of these facets, but *Do-Able Prayer* takes each area and makes a clear case for prayer that impacts them. There is a very helpful blend of biblical teaching with practical illustration for each area.

Do you want to know what it means to abide in Christ? Are you in-terested in protecting your home through prayer? Have you won-dered what it meant to bless others in prayer or struggled with how a congregation can become a praying church? These are the sort of questions that are practically dealt with in every chapter.

I was delighted to discover that Ginny has included insightful discussion questions at the end of each chapter which takes this book from being helpful to an individual and transforms it into a resource that churches can use in small groups and Bible studies. Whether on your own, or in a small group, you will discover just how "do-able" prayer really is!

—Dave Butts
President Harvest Prayer Ministries and National Prayer Committee Chair

Suggestions For Using This Book

The purpose of this book is to see prayer activated across entire congregations and recognized as not for just the passionate few. *Do-Able Prayer* is a fresh, engaging, unexpected approach to simplify everyday prayer. Whether you're a seasoned Prayer Warrior, a Pastor, or a Pilgrim new to prayer, *Do-Able Prayer* will surprise you, encourage you and enlighten you. Walk along this freshly blazed trail with our author and enjoy the journey as she illuminates story after story of how everyday prayer has transformed lives, including her own!

This book is scalable for multiple audiences and can be used in a number of ways.
- Read alone
- Small group and Bible study settings (with dig deeper options)
- Eight week Sermon Series (Sermon outlines being developed) Shorter segments can be preached or taught by selecting the chapter(s) you want to focus on.

SERMON OUTLINE INFORMATION

Sermon Outlines will be available for all the chapters. They are free and are being developed by a group of pastors. As they become available they will be uploaded to http://sermons.logos.com/profile/ginny-kisling. You can also Google "Ginny Kisling's Sermons & Illustrations."

- Whole Church Engagement: Preaching series in conjunction with members reading the book and/or using it in a small group setting

Suggestions for Small Groups
- Pray at the beginning of each meeting time and leave time at the end to practice praying together utilizing the suggestions given at the end of each chapter.

- Rotate the facilitation of the group or choose a facilitator.
- Read and review the key verses identified at the end of the chapter and discuss the application to the chapter.
- Utilize the study questions at the end of each chapter which are designed to promote discussion and learning. In order to get the full effect of this, the goal should be to get through all questions first. If time allows, return to particular questions for continued discussion.
- Encourage participants to highlight significant points in the chapter and include for discussion.
- Utilize the optional "Dig Deeper" section that follows the questions at the end of each chapter. Depending on your level of interest and time you can do as much or as little as desired with this section. If you are studying the book as a group, consider using different translations and reading the Scriptures referenced for each chapter in a round robin style to capture the full flavor of the meaning, intent and connection to the chapter. If you are conducting this study independently, record your observations and look for points in common across the passages as they relate to the chapter or significant points in the chapter.
- Feel free to enhance the group experience with your creativity and the leading of the Holy Spirit. Enjoy!

Best Practice
Pray before you read or use this book. Ask the Holy Spirit to open the eyes of your heart and mind to see and hear what you need most.

Note to Pastors and Teachers
Ideally your message will be a compliment to the chapter in the book. The Sermon Outlines will provide some helpful guidelines.

When I meet with pastors, one question that always gives them great pause is "What would your church be like if everyone was praying?" That is the reason for this book: to see prayer activated across entire congregations, not just the passionate few!

The following section "Chapter Summaries" will be a helpful resource for you as you review the direction and development of the chapters for this book in consideration for how you would like to use this equipping prayer resource in your church.

Chapter Summaries

■ SUMMARY, Chapter 1 –" Five Percenters"
(those passionate-in prayer)

We are all wired differently for prayer, each with his or her own unique role. The *Five Percenters* are people who are passionate-in-prayer, who are given as a protection for the church, and who are behind the scenes equippers for the Body of Christ in the spiritual realm. Their gifts need support and nurture from the church in order for them to thrive in healthful ways. As part of their equipping function, *Five Percenters* prepare the way in prayer for the rest of the Body of Christ.

■ SUMMARY, Chapter 2 – "Ninety-five Percenters"
(the rest of the congregation who are growing in their prayer life)

When we become a believer, we receive *spiritual homesteading* privileges. The Lord has given us each a "field" in which to work. One thing we share in common with one another is having a field of service in prayer. When working together in this field, we are each doing our part in rebuilding the *Wall of Prayer* for our homes, our workplaces, our churches, our cities and the nations.

■ SUMMARY, Chapter 3 –"Abiding – Staying Connected With the Living God"

Abiding in Christ is not about performance or what we can do for Him; it is about a relationship that is engaged in on an ongoing basis. We can be in relationship with Jesus at all times, even in the hectic pace of a given day. Jesus is interceding for us 24/7, stirring up the waters of life and faith for us to step into in any given moment. When we abide in Christ, His fragrance emanates from our life to those around us.

■ SUMMARY, chapter 4 – "Protect and Sanctify Your Home"

Home is where God's heart is. Jesus as a "Wall of Fire" is our greatest spiritual protector (Zechariah 2:5). We can guard against internal intruders by spiritually re-mapping our homes and by raising the volume of spiritual authority through the spoken Word and prayer - all very do-able activities!

■ SUMMARY, chapter 5 – "Turning Your Thoughts Into Prayers" (at Work and School)

Each of us is a designer creation by God. No one is exactly like us or will have the same connections with others that we have. By turning our thoughts into prayers, we can transform our connection points into spiritual *hot spots* of God's activity wherever we go in the natural intersections of life. We can move about freely in prayer as virtual "prayer-mobiles" because we have the influence of our King at our disposal 24/7.

■ SUMMARY, chapter 6 – "Fortifying the Wall of Prayer in Your Church"

A praying life is the *fire-power* for every believer and the church. God has given each person in His church a role of prayer that is perfectly sized for them. As each of us takes our place in prayer, we will begin to put in place impenetrable *Prayer Walls* that guard and keep our churches from harm instead of building friendly fences with poorly protected boundary lines against the enemy. The right amount of *fire-power* will release the church to her true mission and destiny.

■ SUMMARY, chapter 7 – "The Gift of a Spoken Blessing"

The fact that God began the world with a spoken blessing and Jesus closed His earthly ministry with one, underscores for us the power and benefits of words that bless. These two acts of "Spoken Blessings" are well appointed bookends in-time, containing an irrefutable God in display. The baton of blessing has been passed to His children to speak forth His creative blessings into a world hungry for Him.

■ **SUMMARY, chapter 8 – "God's Heart for the Nations"**

No one is a stranger to God. He knows and is profoundly interested in every person He has created. Through his *economy of giving* and *economy of prayer* He seeks to balance the scales of justice in the world. As each of us adds our prayers to the growing chorus of prayer around the world, we become part of the ever-expanding human prayer chain stepping in to God's hotbed of spiritual activity around the globe.

Part One

How We Are Wired

Chapter 1

The Five Percenters

"I learned that success was not about the number of people who attended the prayer time or how much visibility I had in my role . . ."

Who are those strange people who like to pray? You might be surprised to learn that this is a common thought and question held by many. In my experience of prayer ministry leadership, I have found when it comes to prayer there are essentially two broad categories of people. The first group is what I call the *Five Percenters* and the second are the *Ninety-five Percenters*.

Dr. Peter Wagner, former Professor of Church Growth at Fuller Theological Seminary, cited in his book *Prayer Shield* that "5 percent of the church members in the average congregation provide 80 percent of the meaningful intercession." This same observation has been borne out in my experience as well. Everyone knows who these *Five Percenters* are. If there is a need or a crisis, we know exactly who to call. They are loosely referred to as Intercessors and/or Prayer Warriors. Every church has them, and we are grateful for them. They earn their reputation by legitimate behind-the-scenes praying. The other 95 percent are the regular, every day Christians seeking to grow in their prayer life, some of whom have learned the rigorous and exciting disciplines of prayer and are actively engaged in on-going conversations with the Lord. First I want to focus on the *Five Percenters* as I believe it will help to clear up some of the mystery around prayer.

One of my collaborators for this book, Reverend Timothy Vink, of-

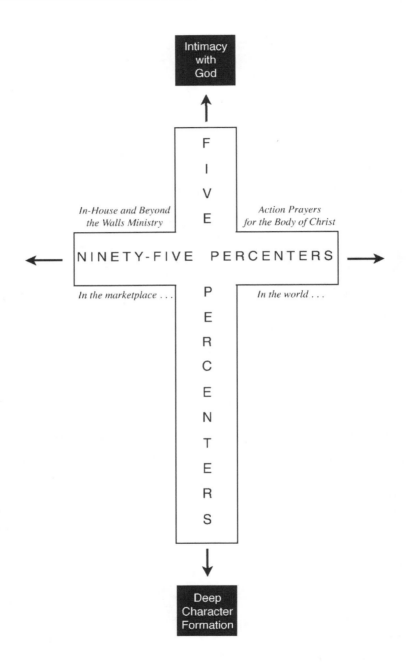

fers valuable insight for the roles of the *Five Percenter* and the *Ninety-Five Percenter* that capture both their uniqueness and their intersection with one another in the Body of Christ. "The cross," he says, "has both a vertical and horizontal axis. *Five Percenters* thrive on the vertical axis . . . UP into intimacy with God for hours, DOWN into deep character formation and conviction from hearing from God. The *Ninety-five Percenters* seem to thrive and live more on the horizontal axis (and dip into the vertical of course) with ACROSS the board ministry and action prayers to the Body of Christ and the world in the marketplace of life."

The Cross illustration on the opposite page captures the relationship God has designed for all of us – interconnected.

My Call to the Prayer Ministry

Eight years into my journey in the world of prayer leadership I was reading in the book of Nehemiah when the Lord impressed me with what would become a strong theme in my prayer ministry call. Just as Nehemiah was called to rebuild the wall in Jerusalem, God was calling me to help in rebuilding the *Wall of Prayer.* This wall would not be rebuilt by pastors and prayer warriors alone, but only as every man, woman, and child of God finds their voice in prayer. It was at this point that I realized the Lord was calling me into a ministry of equipping and mobilization. Not fully understanding just how much disrepair this *wall* was in, I set out with enthusiasm for the journey and became part of a national prayer organization, Harvest Prayer Ministries, which is dedicated to coming alongside churches to assist them in becoming Houses of Prayer.

Initially, I was not sure what shape or form this call would take as the past eight years had not been easy. There had been many discouragements for me along the way. In fact, I had been praying that the Lord would send someone more capable to take my place in leading prayer for my church. In those early years I did not feel very successful in my prayer leadership role. Looking back, I can tell you that I am very thankful God chose to answer my prayer by keeping me right where I was! It can be hard to stay the course when we do not understand the *why* of it. Had I given in to logic and reason, I would not have remained on the scene as Prayer Leader for my church. At the time, all I could see was little attendance at prayer events and feeling invisible in my role, just to name a few frustrations.

What I came to realize was that God's measurement for success is very different from our own. Success was not about the number of people who attended the prayer times or the degree of visibility in my role; rather, it was about my obedience even in the smallest of things, underscoring once again that God's ways are indeed higher than our ways (Isaiah 55:9). He continued to encourage and remind me of the principle in His Word which says that he who is faithful in little will be faithful in much (Luke 16:10).

Thus I continued to muddle and navigate my way through the prayer ministry maze while seeking to learn everything I could from the Lord and others who had travelled this road. Fortunately for me there were many great Christians who had written on prayer. There were also some very gifted current day folks on the scene who had led the way in the world of prayer ministry development and mobilization from whom I could learn.

Wired Differently for Prayer

In those early days I had been trying, without realizing it, to mold myself into one of the *Five Percenters*. But regardless of how many prayer events I attended or led, or how many Prayer Warriors I hung out with, I didn't fit that mold. Despite how many prayer postures I assumed or how many books I read from the great Christians of the past and present, I still could not change the color of my stripes. I simply was not a *Five Percenter*! Over time, I began to see that people are simply wired differently when it comes to prayer, and I did not fall into this group even though I had been called into prayer leadership.

This understanding really hit home for me with one of the strong relationships I had developed. One of my closest friends, Gini, is a bona-fide Intercessor. Gini had assumed that because I was always there to pray and often mobilizing people for prayer, I was just like her when it came to prayer. Though I had come to realize we were different, I did not have the language or understanding at the time to adequately articulate our unlikeness. It took Gini and me five years to realize that she and I are radically different, which we both laugh about today.

To further illustrate the difference between us, let me give you an example of how the two of us would have very disparate responses to a similar situation. When the Lord does something amazing for Gini, the first thing she wants to do is spend time with the Lord - praising Him and praying for deeper understanding of the spiritual aspects of the event. In other words, she goes straight to God's Throne Room. When the Lord does something equally astounding for me, my first response is to convert it to a lesson and shout it out from the Temple steps to anyone who will listen. With this example you can see two completely dissimilar outcomes from two people wired very differently, yet each response is entirely appropriate.

Gini and I did not come by this understanding and acceptance of each other easily. We worked side by side in many prayer ministry venues, both small and large. In these settings Gini was able to see my administrative and mobilization side in action while I was able to see and experience the depth of her intercessory life and spiritual sensitivities at work. Without the benefit of Gini's prayers and spiritual gifts, I am quite certain my effectiveness for God's Kingdom would be dramatically reduced. You see, I am about as far over on the grid for being task driven (there is usually a high level of urgency from my vantage point when I am on task) as one can get. In my natural state, and without the Holy Spirit's intervention, I can be like a bull in a china shop! While the Lord had worked with me on this my entire Christian life, it was in the confines of close-knit ministry relationships that I experienced the most growth.

Eight years into my prayer ministry leadership the Lord added two more members to my up-close-and-personal team who also belong to the *Five Percenter* group. Coincidentally, they each also have the gift of mercy. Starting our meetings together is always a bit comical as the three of them engage in lively chit-chat over the events of the day while I'm off to the side, smiling and tapping my agenda with a pencil. Generally I do the hosting as it gives my task-driven self an acceptable bridge with the happy threesome.

One could draw any number of conclusions about why the Lord chose to put this motley team together, but suffice it to say that over time we have become living, breathing proof of Proverbs 27:17 - "Iron sharpens iron so one man sharpens another." *Our relationships have refined themselves on the anvil of God's grace over the years*, and I am deeply indebted to Gini, Marty, and Marlene, all of whom I have grown to love deeply for their faithfulness to God's call upon their life and their partnership in ministry. They are definitely my up-close and personal *Accountability Team*.

I liken these three modern-day Intercessors/Prayer Warriors to a woman named Anna who is described in Luke 2:37: "Anna never left the temple but worshipped there with fasting and prayer day and night." And while none of my *Accountability Team* actually lives in the church praying and worshipping day and night, each carries the spirit of Anna for worship and prayer, and I am one of the fortunate beneficiaries.

Mystery Surrounding Prayer

Earlier I mentioned that I wanted to clear up some of the mystery surrounding prayer. While prayer comes easily for those in the 5 percent group, it can be more difficult to explain or understand for those who fall into the 95 percent category. The perplexity often deepens as conclusions are drawn about prayer from their encounters with Intercessors and Prayer Warriors along the way.

A frequent comment I hear from people is, "I will leave the praying to the Prayer Warrior," as if the Prayer Warrior has a corner on prayer and there is a *Keep Out* sign for everyone else. Jesus taught us that prayer is for everyone, even giving us great instruction on how to pray by teaching us the Lords' prayer in Matthew 6:9-13. James tells us to pray for one another so that we may be healed and goes on to say that the "prayer of a righteous person is both powerful and effective" (James 5:16).

As prayer becomes more comprehensible and we understand the Intercessor/Prayer Warrior better, more Christians will be encouraged to sojourn with Christ into this school, calling out to Him and experiencing His promise to tell us "great and mighty things" (Jeremiah 33:3). He wants each of us to discover that *our* prayers can be both powerful and effective.

The description of a Prayer Warrior that follows is by no means all-inclusive, nor is it meant to pigeon hole anyone. Even within the prayer community there are differences and varying degrees of these traits. This list is drawn from a combination of sources that include God's Word, conversations I have had with people in both the 5 percent and 95 percent categories, observations I have made over the course of sixteen years of working in hands-on Prayer Leadership, and the distinct influence of my *Accountability Team*.

The Blessings and Characteristics of an Intercessor/Prayer Warrior:

- are designed to "be on guard" and "alert" in the Spirit, providing an invaluable protection for the church as they stand in the gap in prayer (Ezekiel 22:30; Luke 21:36)
- can be counted on to be at appointed prayer times; always among the faithful few
- "anything prayer" is enough to draw them in
- frequently pray long, beautiful flowing prayers
- generally can pray aloud without discomfort, although there are exceptions
- long for everyone to show up for appointed prayer times
- often have the gift of mercy profoundly accompanying their intercessory gifts
- likely to feel at a 30,000 foot elevation spiritually following a prayer time
- enjoy a very intimate relationship with the Lord. When listening to them pray, one may feel as if they have entered a very private conversation
- like to be the recipient of prayer requests
- often end up in prayer leadership roles, more by default than design, which they happily take on
- do not find it uncommon for the Lord to awaken them in the middle of the night or early morning to pray

■ flourish when their intercession is appreciated by the body of Christ (Hebrews 10:24)

■ pray with intensity - "Some are always wrestling in prayer for you, that you may stand firm in all the will of God, matured and fully assured" (Colossians 4:12).

The life of the Intercessor/Prayer Warrior is not without its challenges. Some become discouraged due to being misunderstood and others find themselves struggling with placement in positions not suited to their gifting. And at times those people around them find certain of their characteristic behaviors unsettling. The following list is descriptive of some of the challenges faced by these *Five Percenters* as well as by those around them.

Potential challenges for Intercessors/Prayer Warriors, or for those around them:

■ They are often misunderstood due to differences in use of language and prayer style.

■ Their long prayers may annoy the average pray-er and cause a group rhythm to be lost.

■ Struggling to understand why others do not have the same urgency to join them in prayer can cause them to feel alone and isolated.

■ If placed in leadership positions without the needed administrative and equipping gifts, they may become not only discouraged but distraught.

■ Their intensity and sometimes loud fervency in prayer can be irritating to others. It is especially difficult for some to comprehend the tears, wailing, and even physical manifestations that may take place.

■ They may struggle with their own impatience, being ready to move at warp speed when others are not.

■ An immature Prayer Warrior exhibiting ill-temper or demanding change and seeking to wield ungodly influence can be very unsettling to the Body of Christ.

■ Prayer Warriors who feel unwanted or underappreciated are often tempted to slip away quietly, thereby denying others in the church the much needed protection in prayer they can offer.

Additional Insights into the life of an Intercessor/Prayer Warrior

It is a little known fact that those folks who fit squarely into the Intercessor/Prayer Warrior realm often suffer from discouragement, isolation, loneliness and sometimes depression. Because we historically have understood so little about them in the church, they frequently live under a cloud of their own self-doubt about this form of ministry. Some years ago I read a story about a lady whose husband had her committed to an asylum because all she wanted to do was pray! Oh my, we have come a long way. This was during an era where husbands were legally able to do such things in America. Thankfully over the last few decades there have been many leaders in the Prayer Movement who have given voice to these "Called out" ones and provided venues for them to participate in that affirm them in their praying and place in the Body of Christ (Romans 12:3-8). While I am thankful for the role of the Para Church Ministries, I am also quite certain that the Lord desires for the church at large to receive them with the same grace and affection. We are definitely seeing signs of this in the Bay Area where I live, and where pastors across all denominations gather together for worship and prayer venues on a regular basis.

As Christians, we are called to be *living sacrifices* (Romans 12:1-2). In my experience and observation, prayer could be considered more of a *living sacrifice* for the *Ninety-five Percenters,* who will at times feel like they are lugging a boulder into the Throne Room of God. For the *Five Percenters* however, praying is anything but a sacrifice. They long for it, they thrive in it, they live for it! It is their identity. I have a friend who literally wakes up in the morning with prayers flowing from her lips. The "living sacrifice" for the Intercessor/Prayer Warrior is the discouragement, isolation, loneliness and being misunderstood. This is the price they pay for their service to the Lord. Be encouraged, Intercessor/Prayer Warrior! The Lord understands your life very well; this sacrifice is "your spiritual act of worship which is Holy and pleasing to God" (Romans 12:1-2).

One area that has often led to misunderstanding within the Body of Christ is the nature and calling of an Intercessor/Prayer Warrior as it relates to a specific prayer assignment given them by the Lord. Intercessors will happily take up such an assignment. However, just because they have a passion for prayer, or are in a prayer leadership role, does not automatically mean that they have an *assignment* to pray with on-going and persistent passion for everything that is presented to them. In speaking about this I am not referring to the one-of-a-kind on-the-spot prayer requests that we are to encourage amongst the family of God. However, in my experience and observation, it is often assumed that the person who is passionate-in-prayer will want to pray continuously and relentlessly for every need given them. The mature Intercessor will discern the persistence and duration of their assignment.

Giving explanation to the Intercessor/Prayer Warrior in some detail here is simply meant to help us all understand the responsibility and burden they carry when it comes to prayer. By no means is it meant to discourage anyone from asking for prayer, but we must all be mindful that what is true for the whole Body of Christ is true for them as well; each person needs to be sure that what they are saying "yes" to is in alignment with God's will for their life. I often counsel people to pray on the spot when approached with a prayer need and then ask the Lord if they are to continue to pray for that particular request in the future. We can see this model of prioritizing in alignment with the Father's will clearly demonstrated by Jesus when He said, "I do exactly what my Father has commanded me" (John 14:31). Jesus had clarity about His purpose and His priorities. There was a certainty about the particular people he would spend time with and the places he would go each day. At one point we even see Jesus wisely reminding those he was with to keep their priorities straight in how they allocate their time (Mark 14:7)!

Preparing the Way

God gives gifts to the whole body in order "to prepare God's people for works of service, so that the body may be built up, until we all reach unity in the faith and in the knowledge of the Son of God and become mature, attaining to the whole measure of the fullness of Christ" (Eph. 4:11-13). In my case He has given me an "equipping" gift which I use to help prepare others for the work of prayer. Though invisible and most often behind the scenes, Intercessors and Prayer Warriors also utilize an equipping gift through their fervent and relentless prayers for the Body of Christ. They prepare the ground, spiritually speaking. God has given us people who are passionate-in-prayer to prepare the way for us and elevate us in our ministries by the grace of God at work in them (Romans 12:4-8). Andrew Murray said "There is no great work of God that has ever happened in history that has not first been preceded in prayer." Reverend Daniel Nash (known as Father Nash) understood this first hand. Following six years of pulpit ministry, he became the personal intercessor for Charles Finney, leader in the Second Great Awakening, for the last seven years of his life. He often went into towns a considerable amount of time before Finney was to hold his meetings in order to pray. Father Nash would pray before, during, and after the meetings, and the reported retention rate for new believers was said to be around 80 percent. This is a clear case where a powerful intercessor, Father Nash, equipped Charles Finney in the realm of the spirit by way of prayer. It has been reported that Charles Spurgeon always had someone in the basement praying while he preached. My personal intercessory team equips me for the work of ministry through their work of intercession on my behalf. When these folks intercede in this way, they are doing so in accordance with the measure of faith given to them by the Lord Himself (Romans 12:3).

There is a beautiful remote peninsula located in Mount Athos, Greece, that is commonly referred to as the Holy Mount. It is home to twenty monasteries that are completely dedicated to prayer and the worship of the Lord Jesus Christ. In fact, uninterrupted prayers have been offered there by the resident monks for over one thousand years! Totally dedicated to prayer, the monks sleep only a few hours every day and eat just two meals per day. Once they arrive at Mount Athos, it is for life. They never leave the island, which itself is completely self-sustaining. All the monks participate in growing and harvesting the food. There is an on-site medical doctor who is rarely busy as there is remarkably little cancer and heart disease among the monks.

One of the prayers the monks can be heard repeating as they go about their daily routine is "Lord Jesus, have mercy on me." Their day begins at sunset (they operate according to Byzantine time), and every day at 3:00 a.m. they stop praying on their own and are summoned to the church to pray for eight hours corporately. The monks refer to this time as an eight hour conversation with God, a dress rehearsal for eternity. Their single-minded focus and passion is to move closer to Christ every day. When you hear about this kind of life, you are likely to think it is the epitome of self-sacrifice and wonder how anyone can exist this way. Surprisingly though, there is a long waiting list. In fact, it is harder to get into a Mount Athos monastery than to be accepted into Harvard!

What is even more amazing is that the prayers the monks offer at Mount Athos are not influenced by world events or news of the day. They do not have TV, radio, newspapers or access to news of the outside world in any way. Consequently there is little distraction or temptation to spend their time on speculations that are common to most of us. Every major news event that happens in our world is filled with talking heads both reporting and speculating. A lot of air space is given to meaningless chatter. The monks, however, have chosen a life of consecration and believe that by prayer they are affecting the world, blessing and doing battle against forces of darkness every day. (See "End Notes" for website addresses to learn more about Mount Athos).

We can truly thank God for all the Prayer Warriors around the world. Their role has a deeper and wider berth in the spiritual realm than many of us may understand. They are tending to spiritual battles in ways that the average person may not even be aware of or realize is needed. We know from God's Word that "Our struggle is not against flesh and blood, but against the rulers, against the authorities, against the powers of this dark world and against the spiritual forces of evil in the heavenly realm" (Ephesians 6:12). Many Prayer Warriors I know believe that they are actively doing spiritual battle on others' behalf and taking down strongholds in the spiritual realm by their relentless and strategic prayer. In their own way, modern day Prayer Warriors are like the monks of Mount Athos whose continuing prayers are guarding the church and the land in the spiritual realm. They are wielding their spiritual machetes to whack away the dark underbrush, so to speak, so that you and I can come into the Throne Room of God a little easier and do the work of ministry without as much interference. Without a doubt, strategically placed Prayer Warriors are essential to the advancement of the Kingdom. "Some are always wrestling in prayer for you, that you may stand firm in all the will of God, matured and fully assured" (Colossians 4:12). Indeed, the world owes much to the fervent, believing prayers of such Intercessors.

It is important for the pastor and church leadership to understand the value and calling of Intercessors and Prayer Warriors and seek to nurture and support those relationships in order that they function in healthful ways for the Body of Christ. These *Five Percenters* are one of the protections and extraordinary blessings that the Lord has provided for the church (Isaiah 62:6; Ezekiel 33:6).

Do-Able Prayers
■ Lord, thank you for the Intercessors/Prayer Warriors you have given to the church and the nations who have gone before us to prepare the way.

■ Lord, forgive me for any lack of appreciation I may have had or displayed for those who are passionate-in-prayer.

■ Lord, thank you for the sacrifice of the Intercessors/Prayer Warriors as they labor on others' behalf. Bless and comfort them in their times of loneliness and isolation.

IN SUMMARY – Chapter 1
We are all wired differently for prayer, each with his or her own unique role. The *Five Percenters* are people who are passionate-in-prayer, who are given as a protection for the church, and who are behind the scenes equippers for the Body of Christ in the spiritual realm. Their gifts need support and nurture from the church in order for them to thrive in healthful ways. As part of their equipping function, *Five Percenters* prepare the way in prayer for the rest of the Body of Christ.

Key Verses: Ephesians 4:11-13, Romans 12:3-8, Luke 2:36-37

STUDY/DISCUSSION/REFLECTION QUESTIONS

1. How does your childhood experience with prayer influence your prayer life today?

2. Based on the description for the two categories, do you believe you belong to the *5 Percent* or *95 Percent* group? Why?

3. What category is Anna in (Luke 2:36-37)? Elaborate.

4. In what kind of situations might prayer be uncomfortable for you or for others?

5. Why do you think prayer gatherings draw such small numbers?

6. How are Intercessors/Prayer Warriors equippers in the Body of Christ?

7. In what ways are you like, or unlike, a Prayer Warrior?

8. What is the *living sacrifice* for an Intercessor/Prayer Warrior?

9. Write down anything new that you learned about the characteristics of an Intercessor/Prayer Warrior.

Use this opportunity to pray together utilizing the *Do-Able Prayers* in this chapter.

DIG DEEPER - Optional; refer to suggestions page

These passages were referenced in this chapter: *Isaiah 55:9; Luke 16:10; Proverbs 27:17; Luke 2:37; Matthew 6:9-13; James 5:16; Jeremiah 33:3; Ezekiel 22:30; Luke 21:36; Hebrews 10:24; Colossians 4:12; Romans 12:3-8; Romans 12:1-2; John 14:31; Mark 14:7; Eph. 4:11-13; Romans 12:4-8; Isaiah 62:6; Ezekiel 33:6*

Chapter 2

The Ninety-five Percenters

*"Do-Able Prayer is praying in a way that fits you –
who you are and how you are wired."*

After reading about the *Five Percenters* in the first chapter, you may feel a sigh of relief knowing that when you became a Christian you were not automatically required to become a Prayer Warrior. On the other hand, you may be one of the *Five Percenters* who are perplexed that so many others in the church do not care about prayer to the extent that you do - or at least it seems that way. In either case, this chapter is for you! The message in it comes around full circle to help both groups understand one another better and remove some common misperceptions about prayer and people's approach to it.

Who are the Ninety-five Percenters?

First let me say that while I have lumped everyone else together into the category of the *Ninety-five Percenters*, there are any number of folks within this broad category who, like myself, have personally grown in prayer disciplines and their love of prayer and can be regularly seen joining in with their brothers and sisters in Christ in prayer. However, understanding some of the challenges and differences for people in both groups can be very helpful and instructive for the Body of Christ. So no matter where you find yourself in your prayer growth continuum, this information can be helpful, maybe even eye-opening for you.

So who are the *Ninety-five Percenters*? For the purpose of this discussion, they represent those who do not consider themselves Intercessors and/or Prayer Warriors, which would apply to the majority of believers. And if this majority still needs to find their voice in prayer, then we have a huge gap in the spiritual power base of our churches. Can you imagine running an engine on only 5 percent of its power, or receiving just 5 percent of your electricity? What if a sunny day consisted of only 5 percent of the sun's rays filtering through to earth? Or think about waking up and having available only 5 percent of the physical energy that you normally require for the day? You might get by with such a small amount of these essentials for a short time, but it certainly is not sustainable. Let's just say, for the sake of argument, that 50 percent of the Christian population is somewhat active in prayer. That is still only half the fuel and power available to the church for her mission. If you were the owner of a business and your staff was working at 50 percent capacity, you would be doing everything possible to get more productivity out of them or face the closure of your business. Is it any wonder that we are seeing so many churches close their doors each year?

In speaking with many folks who see themselves in the *95 Percent* group, I have discovered that they have had one or more of the following thoughts or experiences when it comes to prayer: (check the ones you can relate to)

❑ have heard a Prayer Warrior praying and knew they could never pray that way

❑ attended a prayer meeting where the majority of the time was spent taking requests for prayer and only a few minutes were actually spent in prayer

❑ could not relate to the given prayer request: someone's grandmother's neighbor's grandson's brother hurt himself at work, and on it goes....

❑ couldn't make the connection between praying and God's answers

❑ believe that prayer is mainly for a crisis

❑ not sure that God would hear *their* prayers, even if they tried

❑ do not want to bother God with personal requests

❑ do not feel confident enough to pray aloud for fear of stumbling over their words

❑ feel satisfied with their prayer life and consider it to be more of a private matter

❑ prayer is important and they need to do it more

❑ would like their prayers to be powerful and effective

❑ want to grow in learning how to pray in simple do-able ways that work for how they are wired and with their lifestyle

If you can relate to any of the aforementioned items, you are not alone. Many I have spoken with have experienced one or more of the items on this list and, as a result, have settled for leaving the serious praying to the Prayer Warriors, even though they may feel a twinge of guilt about doing so.

Do-Able Prayer is all about praying in a way that fits *you* - who you are and how you are wired. It is praying in a way that fits your Kingdom call so that you can be counted among those who are rebuilding the *Wall of Prayer* in our land. If you are experiencing any guilt or fear about your prayer life, I pray that you will be able to let go and replace these negative emotions with anticipation for learning more about *Do-Able Praying*.

Spiritual Homesteading

What Christians often do not realize is that when they became believers, they were automatically given *spiritual homesteading* privileges. Think of the American settlers who came out West and were given a plot of land to work. They had a set of conditions to meet in order to maintain ownership of that land. For example, they had to live on and work the land. If they abandoned their land, even for a short while, they lost their legal rights to it and someone else could come in and lay claim. You are the legal owner of the spiritual climate in your sphere of influence, thus your *spiritual homesteading* privileges. But just like the early settlers who moved out West, you have to work your claim in prayer in order to retain your legal rights over the spiritual territory the Lord has given you. This idea of working a claim in prayer may be completely new to you or even seem a bit odd. But be assured that, just like the inexperienced early day homesteaders, you can set out with their same determination *and,* with God's help, stake and retain your spiritual claim over your unique spheres of influence. Paul encourages us that "Each one should retain the place in life that the Lord assigned to him and to which God has called him" (1 Corinthians 7:17). Our spheres of influence are one application of the places in which God has called us, and asserting prayer is how we gain, retain and build our position of spiritual authority in the traffic and intersections of our lives. God anoints where He appoints. "A man can receive only what is given him from heaven" (John 3:27).

Rees Howells, a humble servant of the Lord from Wales, is a great example of someone whose "homesteading" in prayer throughout his life had a great effect in his time and place. The book *Rees Howells, Intercessor* written by Norman Percy Grubb has greatly encouraged me as I have read and re-read it over the years. It is an inspirational true story of a passionate-in-prayer Welshman whom God raised up out of the coal mines in Wales in the early twentieth century for a powerful purpose. In 1920, Rees and his wife had just come off the mission field from Africa and begun a very successful worldwide speaking tour underwritten by their mission headquarters. It was during one such speaking engagement at Moody Bible Institute in Chicago that the Lord settled in Rees's mind that He wanted him to build a Bible College in Wales. Through a series of miraculous events, the Bible College opened in 1924.

For years Rees had been a man with a world vision. Then in 1935 the Lord gave him the "Every Creature Vision," meaning that every creature in the world was to hear the gospel of Christ. Rees Howells would work fervently the rest of his days to see this vision fulfilled.

It is a little known fact that through his work and ministry, the Bible College of Wales was instrumental in using the power of unrelenting, strategic prayer to affect events of World War II. It is reported that in the early days of the conflict the Lord told Rees that the war was necessary, for without it the three great dictators - Hitler, Mussolini, and Stalin - would override the world. At the time, Hitler was boasting of setting up a Nazi regime throughout the world which would last for a thousand years. In her book *The Intercession of Rees Howells*, Ms. Doris Ruscoe, former Headmistress of the school for missionaries' children founded by Rees Howells, says "As each crisis in the war developed, the Holy Spirit guided our prayers, and each time we knew that victory had been gained in the spirit before news came over the radio or in the newspapers of victory on the field of battle." Many key victories were won in prayer during this time. Moscow did not fall, and the attack on Britain in the autumn of 1940 failed and the invasion did not take place.

In February of 1950, Rees went home to be with the Lord and his son Samuel took over his father's work. Samuel died in 2004 and the campus was subsequently moved to Rugby, Warwickshire in England and has been renamed Trinity School of Theology. (See end notes for book and internet site information).

As I was reviewing the story of Rees Howells again for this book, I sensed the Holy Spirit asking me a most unusual question. "Was Rees an Intercessor?" My first thought was that it was an odd question since the only two books written about him referred to him in their titles as an Intercessor. Often I find that the Lord will ask me a question to cause me to prayerfully consider an additional thought around a particular subject, and this turned out to be the case here. I was to discover that the Holy Spirit's question was not so much for the purpose of examining Rees and his life of intercession as it was to get my attention. My question then became, "Why, Lord, are you asking me this question?" I was a little surprised at the answer He pressed into my mind. "Everything I asked my servant Rees to do - every act of obedience - could *only* be accomplished by prayer and intercession and long uninterrupted times with me." Wow! This really set my mind to thinking. Rees had also been a powerful evangelist, having had great success on the mission field in Africa and in earlier days and places as well. He was also a sought after inspirational speaker and became an extraordinary business man as he built a Bible College that would have a world-wide effect through its graduating students over many years.

So what was the Lord trying to say to me? I believe He wanted me to understand that there is a "field of service" to which He calls some of His children, the breadth of which can only be accomplished by prayer and intercession and long uninterrupted times in His presence. This is a different "field of service" than the one for those who are primarily hidden in the prayer closet as we see with many *5 Percenters*. These "sent" ones come out of the *95 Percent* group, and one of their "must have" activities for successfully fulfilling their call is intercession. So we could say that intercession is an activity for the *95 Percenters* as opposed to the *5 Percent* group who are more inclined to find that intercession is their identity. I began to wonder, "Who are some examples of people described in this way?"

The Apostle Paul is one person who comes to mind. Paul was a great Apostle who was also a giant in prayer. He was a man of action, a "sent one" as we all are sent into the world with the gospel. Being a tentmaker, he also understood being a businessman and a market-place minister in his day. In his book *Praying Like Paul*, speaker and writer Jon Graf says, "Paul knew that prayer truly affected the kingdom; that prayer brought results; that prayer did something in the heavenlies that moved the hand of God and beat back the kingdom of darkness's attempt to thwart his ministry." Indeed Paul knew that in order to carry out the earthly assignment the Lord had given him, his life would have to be transformed by the Savior day-by-day and hour by hour. A lot was riding on it. Paul also knew that he needed the prayers of others and actively engaged the churches to pray for him (2 Corinthians 1:8-11).

Israel's Kings also had extraordinary earthly assignments. Over a six month period I have been soaking up a great little book called *Pray Like the King* by David and Kim Butts, President and Co-founder of Harvest Prayer Ministries. Israel's Kings were also sent ones whose important life stories give us many lessons for praying. One of the kings featured in this book is King Asa who ruled Judah for a total of forty one years. Though Asa did not finish well - his final six years being marked by defiance - he demonstrated very strong leadership capabilities in all the other years. Early on Asa began a national cleansing from the sins of his leader predecessors who tolerated idols and altars to pagan gods. Asa fearlessly tore them down and "commanded Judah to seek the Lord, the God of their fathers, and to obey his laws and commands" (2 Chronicles 14:4). David and Kim Butts note that "His rule was marked by stability and spiritual revival in the nation and that in addition to putting away evil, he also pointed the nation in the right direction." King Asa's years of success required him to be a strong man of prayer who spent much time in God's presence allowing His powerful transforming life to be at work in him.

In the case of Paul and King Asa, their lives were not their own. Once called by God, their days were anything but typical or normal, as we say. Out of love for God, they yielded themselves to the will of the Father, carrying out extraordinary responsibilities which required on-going face time with the Lord.

Paul encourages us in 2 Corinthians 10:13-18 to work the field that God has given to each of us. He is clear to point out that where we work is based on God's assignment, just as the outcomes also belong to the Lord. Understanding the Biblical perspective for our assignment will give us a healthy balance in our view of self and service. One thing we all share in common is that we have been given a "field of prayer" assignment (James 5:16; 1 Thessalonians 5:17; Galatians 6:2; 2 Corinthians 1:8-11). One need not always be a prayer giant to work in their "field of prayer," just one who is available and willing. God Himself will complete what He begins. "The one who calls you is faithful and he will do it" (1 Thessalonians 5:24).

Overcoming a Common Barrier to Prayer

Even with the trail being blazed for us by Intercessors and Prayer Warriors around the world, there is one common barrier that I see surfacing time and again which brings discouragement to the prayer life of believers. It's a belief that their prayers can't possibly make a difference in the big picture. Over time this way of thinking erodes one's confidence in God's character and results in some Christians resigning themselves to powerless living and mediocre spiritual lives. This kind of sustained belief can keep a person from entering into one of the most important partnerships God has designed for us – the partnership of prayer that promotes our spiritual vitality and well-being.

Obviously such thinking isn't true of every believer, but neither is it uncommon. You might be wondering how this has happened. How did we get here? *Why* is this so common? I don't know a Christian alive who would tell you that they want to live a defeated spiritual life! If this particular barrier to praying does not apply to you, you likely know someone to whom it does, and who is suffering as a result. Perhaps you are that person. If so, don't be discouraged. The problem is quite fixable!

Let's begin to take this apart in a very simple way by examining the thought "my prayers can't possibly make a difference." There is nothing humble about this thought. In fact, it is the opposite of humility because it arises out of "self-focus." This kind of belief is an easy trap to fall into because our early prayer life is generally centered on our needs or on praying in a crisis. While this is completely natural, left unchecked over time this limited, finite lens makes it difficult to imagine an inspired outcome that would have any significant *Kingdom* impact. The resulting belief can easily become "My prayers can't possibly make a difference." And, of course, this is just what the enemy would have you believe.

God's Truth Will Set Us Free!

God's Word tells us that His truth will set us free (John 8:32). Terry Teykl, noted author and speaker, has a great understanding of prayer. One that, if you will take it to heart, will never again leave you disappointed with the outcome of your prayers. "The purpose of prayer," he says, "is to conform us to the image of Christ." As long as we believe that our prayer effectiveness is somehow fueled by our abilities or our self-worth we will not have much of a prayer life. We will come to the end of self rather quickly. The truth is that *God* is the Great Initiator of Prayer. We only know Him because He first loved us and drew us unto Himself (John 3:16). While He beckons us to continue to talk to Him about the things that concern us, His ultimate goal is to draw us into a deeper relationship with Him where we begin to care about what is on His heart for His world. It is from this position He can then initiate prayer within us so that we are praying at *His* prompting. This kind of relationship results in a partnership with us that brings His transforming power into our everyday lives for His good will and pleasure (Philippians 2:13; Luke

2:14). It is a partnership without limits because God sits outside of time and space... (just imagine what that could mean). Once we understand the dynamic of this partnership, we are set free from a belief system that convinces us that the effectiveness and results of our prayers are tied to our worth and our ability. No longer are we left to pray only from our imagination! Now our prayers, initiated by Him, are becoming part of carrying out the will of the Father into His earth. The truth that sets us free is that it is by *His* power and partnership that our prayers make a difference in the world (Zechariah 4:6; Ephesians. 3:20).

Well known author and pastor Max Lucado says in his book *He Still Moves Stones*, "...the power of prayer is in the One who hears it and-not the one who says it..." If this applies to you and you are ready for this kind of partnership with the Lord, why not speak with Him right now? Let Him know that you have had faulty thinking but now want His truth to set you completely free! Can you say AMEN with me?

Do-Able Prayer is for Everyone

In chapter 1 we discussed the role of Intercessors and Prayer Warriors, many of whom spend a form of continuous prayer before the Lord. Of course, the 24/7 approach to prayer is not practical or very do-able for the average person. Nor is it wise to try to change your stripes as I tried so hard to do in my earlier years. So, if you are not a Prayer Warrior, the question really becomes, "How do I find my voice in prayer so that it counts for the Kingdom?" As I mentioned earlier in this chapter, I believe you *can*, and I have complete confidence that most Christians desire for their prayers to be both powerful and effective. If you are a person who has found his or her voice in prayer, then you likely already know the fruit of prayer, and I celebrate with you! Therefore, I pray that no matter where you are on the prayer continuum, you will be inspired, as you work your way through this book, to find some new bite-size, do-able ways to pray that you can add into your everyday life.

And for those who are new to finding their voice in prayer, let me assure you that the result can be awesome for you! Discovering your part in rebuilding the *Wall of Prayer* is no less important than what the Prayer Warriors do as they take up their spiritual machetes on our behalf. There are Houses of Prayer and other ministry venues scattered across America and the world today that have risen up to offer uninterrupted prayer. They have gone before us and are praying for us. They have cleared the spiritual underbrush so that we can walk easier in our prayer terrain.

As already mentioned in chapter one, prayer is one of the *living sacrifices* for many of the *Ninety-five Percenters*. It does not always come with ease and can be a challenge for highly actionable people to steady themselves long enough for a conversation with the Lord. But the muscles of prayer can be developed over time with do-able steps. While some are not called to pray day and night or with unrelenting persistence, we can all learn to release our prayer voice according to God's rhythmic timing. In doing so, a choir of prayer sounded by God's children everywhere will continuously be lifted up to rock heaven so powerfully that I'm convinced God's ears will burn. And when God hears, He acts! Revelation 5:8 speaks about the "Golden Bowls of Incense" that symbolize the prayers of the Saints rising to God. May it be so, Lord! May it be so!

Do-Able Prayers
■ Lord, show me the "field of prayer" that you have designed just for me (1 Corinthians 7:17; 2 Corinthians 1:8-11).

■ Lord, help me to develop my prayer muscles so I can do my part in rebuilding the *Wall of Prayer* (James 5:16; Galatians 6:2).

■ Lord, help me to assert prayer in a way that will help me gain, retain and build my position of spiritual authority in the traffic and intersections of my life (1 Thessalonians 5:17).

IN SUMMARY – chapter 2
When we become a believer, we receive *spiritual homesteading* privileges. The Lord has given us each a "field" in which to work. One thing we share in common with one another is having a field of service in prayer. When working together in this field, we are each doing our part in rebuilding the *Wall of Prayer* for our homes, our workplaces, our churches, our cities and the nations.

Key Verses: 1 Corinthians 7:17; 2 Corinthians 10:13-18; 2 Corinthians 1:8-11

STUDY/DISCUSSION/REFLECTION QUESTIONS

1. Have you ever found yourself thinking that you prefer to leave prayer to the Prayer Warriors? How might you be encouraged to think differently after reading this chapter?

2. Discuss how the items you checked earlier in the chapter have impacted your prayer life.

3. Does it make any difference to you to know that you can pray effectively using your own style? How might that affect your prayer life?

4. Would it change anything for you to know that, when you pray, you are part of rebuilding the *Wall of Prayer* in your church, neighborhood, city, and across the nation? If so, what is an example of that change?

5. What do you think compelled Paul and King Asa to develop such strong prayer lives?

6. What is *spiritual homesteading*? Give an example of how one would do this?

7. What is one "field of service" that we all have in common?

8. What is your definition of prayer? How alike or different is it from Terry Teykl's?

9. Read: Romans 15:30; 2 Corinthians 1:11; 1 Timothy 2:1-2; James 5:13-14; James 5:16. Who is being addressed in these passages? What do these passages have in common?

Use this opportunity to pray together using the *Do-Able Prayers* in this chapter.

DIG DEEPER - Optional; refer to suggestions page

These passages were referenced in this chapter: *1 Corinthians 7:17; John 3:27; 2 Corinthians 1:8-11; 2 Chronicles 14:4; 2 Corinthians 10:13-18; James 5:16; 1 Thessalonians 5:17; Galatians 6:2; 1 Thessalonians 5:24; John 8:32; John 3:16; Philippians 2:13; Luke 2:14; Zechariah 4:6; Ephesians. 3:20; Revelation 5:8; 1 Corinthians 7:17; James 5:16; Galatians 6:2*

Part Two

Do-Able Prayers for Your Sphere of Influence

Chapter 3

Abiding - Staying Connected With the Living God

"We are not to be peddlers of God's word but people of sincerity who are commissioned by God, and when we have found our place of abiding with Christ, the fragrance of Christ is spread by us."

(Ginny Kisling – a blended paraphrase of Biblical principles and scripture)

Recently I met with a pastor who shared that he had missed his customary morning prayer time with the Lord due to an unforeseen schedule conflict. He went on to tell me that this occurrence led him to question what it might be like for the people in his church and other Christians when they, too, miss regular times of prayer. Would they struggle with feeling out of sync and slightly "off" for the day? As we mulled this over, we explored what the Lord might have to say. Must we experience a disconnect with ourselves or a sense of things not being quite right just because we occasionally miss our usual prayer appointment with the Lord? How can we remain connected all the time?

One Formula that Works!

Whether or not we miss a set appointment with the Lord on any given day does not change the fact that Jesus came to live among us and to form a unique relationship with us. John 1:14 tells us that "The Word became flesh and dwelt among us." God did not simply send us a manual to live by. He sent us the living text in the form of His Son, Jesus Christ. By the very nature of His relationship with us,

He has set the stage so that you and I can remain vitally connected to Him. Relying on formulas can sometimes get us in trouble, but here is a promise from God's Word that is simple, straightforward, and works without fail: "If we abide in Christ, He abides in us" (John 15:4). The Greek meaning for the word "abide" is to remain, to continue, to stay. Abiding has to do with the concept of *being* rather than *doing,* which is not an easy accomplishment for overscheduled Americans or task-driven Type A personalities. Let's look a little more closely at what it means to abide...

Definitions of "abide"
To wait for; await
To endure without yielding; withstand
To bear patiently; endure
To remain in one place

Synonyms (strict and slang) for "abide":
To stay, dwell, remain
To hang around, stick around
Tarry

In Silicon Valley where I live, "hanging out," "sticking around," or "tarrying" without an agenda is almost unheard of. If one wants to survive and get ahead, multi-tasking is the name of the game in most sectors of the population. In fact, "tarrying without an agenda" is another name for "loitering," and violators may be prosecuted to the full extent of the law!

So how does abiding with Christ fit into these meanings?

A Relationship Renewed in Maui

Abiding is about being in relationship with Christ, and the relationship is more important than the things we do or don't do. This truth was driven home to me earlier in my Christian life when the Lord took my family to live in Maui for nineteen months. We had just come off an intensive time of ministry where our lives had been filled with doing many good things for Him, but I was on the verge of serious burnout from the intensity and non-stop ministry commitments.

When I first arrived in Maui, I immediately put into motion plans for getting involved in the work of the Lord. But something was very wrong. I began to enter a season of spiritual dryness such as I had never known before. It was as if I'd arrived in the wilderness instead of the place of peace and rest I associated with Maui. Accompanying this was a complete lack of energy which soon forced me to withdraw from everything I had signed up for. This was a harsh adjustment for me, and only when the swirl of activity ceased did I begin to understand that this dry season had its particular purpose and that *where I was* would be vital to *where I was going.*

A shocking first revelation was that God, in removing me from ministry for a season, was removing *from* me a false sense of security - one based on ministry accomplishments. He hadn't at all minded that I drew great satisfaction from my teaching, writing, and various other gifts and abilities, but He drew the line at seeing the shift to my trusting in these things as the source of my self-worth. He wanted to be the focal point, the centerpiece of my life. Thus He began to firmly root my security in Him.

I settled into life on Maui which, by most peoples' standards, was enviable. I managed a small resort with the ocean right outside our door and spending my days caring for the lovely grounds provided a much-needed tonic for my weary body, soul, and spirit. Long, leisurely walks on the beach and meeting people from around the world worked miracles of rejuvenation. Without the external demands of ministry, I fell into a new rhythm with the Lord that was filled with a joyful flow of continuous communication. As long as I *abided* with Jesus and kept my eyes fixed on Him, my life on Maui was nurturing and healing. A new level of intimacy was developing with my Lord.

Even so, something happened regularly that was perplexing to me. At some point in my daily communications with the Lord, He would ask, "Am I enough?" Without hesitation I would reply, "Yes, Lord, You are enough." This exchange became a daily ritual for us. Needless to say, I was puzzled. One day, many months into my stay on

Maui and when I was feeling stronger and more spiritually revived, I asked the Lord, "Why do You continue to ask, 'Am I enough?' Haven't I answered that question to your satisfaction?" Surprisingly, He answered with yet another set of questions.

By this point in my life I had learned to know the Lord's voice. He tells us plainly that His sheep hear His voice and follow Him (John 10:27). And what I heard in His next round of questions revealed His longing for me to understand what it actually means that He is with me at every turn, in every situation in life. "Ginny," I heard, "am I enough for you if I do not return to you any of your former gifts, talents, and abilities? Am I enough for you if I do not return you home?" "Am I enough," he continued, "if I do not restore your friendships or your ministry...or your marriage?" This time there was only silence on my part. I had no quick answer, but I finally understood the depth and meaning of His questions. I was to look deep within and ask myself, "Do I really believe He is sufficient for all my needs? He calls Himself the "I AM." What does that mean to me?" I knew He hoped my answer would be, "Lord, You are whatever I need at any point in my life, and I long to know and stay connected to You at a deep heart level. I want to experience more and more of how 'enough' You are." And that would eventually be my answer.

During my times of meditation and contemplation on Maui, I learned to offer up very simple *Do-Able* prayers that helped keep me in the place of abiding. Frequent reading of His Word restored a moisture to my life, keeping me refreshed and encouraged. We are not to be peddlers of God's Word but people of sincerity who are commissioned by Him, and when we have found our place of *ABIDING* with Christ, the fragrance of Christ is spread by us, for we are to God the aroma of Christ and we carry the fragrance of life (1 Corinthians 2:14-17; Psalm 138). Here are some do-able prayers that I offered up frequently during my stay on Maui.

Do-Able Prayers for Abiding
- Lord, have mercy on me (Psalm 86:3).
- Lord, impart your thoughts to me (1 Corinthians 2:10; Isaiah 55:8).

■ Lord, help me to take every thought captive to you (2 Corinthians 10:5).

■ Lord, test and examine my ways (Lamentations 3:40; Jeremiah 17:10).

■ Lord, make my desires your desires (Psalm 37:4).

■ Lord, help me to be faithful in small things (Luke 16:10).

■ Lord, show me which way I should turn today (Isaiah 30:21).

■ Lord, keep me in your dwelling place (Psalm 84:1).

■ Lord, keep me on track today (Philippians 3:12-16).

■ Lord, give me your mind (1 Corinthians 2:16).

■ Lord, help me to set my mind on things above (Colossians 3:2).

■ Lord, help my speech to be gracious (Colossians 4:6).

■ Lord, keep me in your shelter and give me your rest (Psalm 91:1).

■ Lord, more of you and less of me (John 3:30).

Jesus our Ultimate Model

Jesus is our ultimate model for *abiding*. He was always in the place of abiding with His Father when he was on earth. At one point, when His anxious parents were looking for Him, He asked, "Did you not know that I must be about my Father's business" (Luke 2:49; John 14:31)? Truly, one can only be about God's business if they are in a place of abiding.

At a recent Pastors' Prayer Breakfast we broke into small groups to pray for one another. As I was praying for one of the pastors, the Lord brought to my mind's eye an image of the Pool of Bethesda. You may recall this pool from John chapter five and how it was renowned for its curative powers. As I continued to gaze into this mental image in prayer, I could see the pool located right next to the left arm of this pastor. In fact, the pastor was as close to the pool as he could possibly be without jumping right in. As I allowed the Lord to increase my understanding of this image, I could see the Holy Spirit busily stirring the waters and welcoming the pastor in. What I saw next was the pastor's right side conducting his ministry work uninterrupted while at the same time his left side, which was barely touching the water, was receiving all the refreshment and benefit needed. There was no need for him to stop what he was doing for this to happen.

We can see in this vision a great present day application for ourselves because of the intercession of Jesus. Did you know that He is interceding for us all the time? Yesterday, today and tomorrow? The prophet Isaiah referred to the Messiah's intercession in Isaiah 53:12, and He continues in intercession for each of us individually, stirring up the waters of our faith. He speaks into the Father's ear on our behalf around the clock. Yes, even now (Hebrews 7:24-25; Romans 8:34)! Just as the Holy Spirit was engaged in rousing the curative powers in Bethesda's waters, Jesus is busy stirring up the waters of faith and life in us with His continuous intercession. And even as we go about our day-to-day responsibilities, we can enter into that miraculous place of *abiding* and receive the full benefits of the water of life He is moving for us right where we are!

Consider taking a private moment for yourself right now and close your eyes. Imagine yourself at the Pool of Bethesda and thank Jesus for interceding on your behalf to God the Father. Tell Him that you want to wade into His stirred up waters of faith and life. Express your desire to abide with Him. If you ask, I guarantee that a divine connection will happen for you because of God's promise to abide in us if we abide in him (John 15:4).

Steps for Abiding

■ Use any number of the do-able prayers listed in this chapter for abiding or create your own. Another useful step could be writing them on note cards and placing them in strategic places.

■ Do your best to make a daily appointment with the Lord. Celebrate small beginnings; every sincere beginning equals Kingdom advancement. If this is new for you, you might start by setting aside two minutes a day to be with Jesus; the important thing is not *when* you do it but *that* you do it. Seek to make it a habit. You wouldn't leave your home without brushing your teeth or combing your hair, so begin to think of your meeting with the Lord as an equally important and do-able necessity (Zechariah 4:10).

■ Another do-able and significant step for *abiding* is to intentionally decrease so that He may increase. There are times when we need to deliberately take some time apart from our busy schedule and recede, decrease, and simply take ourselves out of the equation. This will exalt the Lord and invite an increase of His presence. If you are struggling to get into the place of abiding, this can be a serious first step (John 3:30).

IN SUMMARY – chapter 3

Abiding in Christ is not about performance or what we can do for Him; it is about a relationship that we engage in on an ongoing basis. We can be in relationship with Jesus at all times, even in the hectic pace of a given day. Jesus is interceding for us 24/7, stirring up the waters of life and faith for us to step into in any given moment. When we abide in Christ, His fragrance emanates from our life to those around us.

Key Verses: John 15:1-8

STUDY/DISCUSSION/REFLECTION QUESTIONS

1. How would you answer this question from the Lord, "Am I enough?"

2. What are your thoughts about the fact that Jesus is always praying for you to God the Father?

3. What kinds of things do you think Jesus might be saying?

4. How simple or hard do you think it is to abide? Why?

5. What benefits do you think might result from abiding?

6. Have you ever had a time in your spiritual journey when "where you were was vital to where you were going?" Share an example.

7. Choose a prayer from the Do-Able Prayer list in this chapter and pray over the person on your left in your group by inserting their name. Example: "Lord impart your thoughts to John this week."

DIG DEEPER - Optional; refer to suggestions page

These passages were referenced in this chapter: *John 1:14; John 15:4; John 10:27; 1 Corinthians 2:14-17; Psalm 138; Psalm 86:3; 1 Corinthians 2:10; Isaiah 55:8; 2 Corinthians 10:5; Lamentations 3:40; Jeremiah 17:10; Psalm 37:4; Luke 16:10; Isaiah 30:21; Psalm 84:1; Philippians 3:12-16; 1 Corinthians 2:16; Colossians 3:2; Colossians 4:6; Psalm 91:1; John 3:30; Luke 2:49; John 14:31; John 5; John 15:4; Zechariah 4:10; John 3:30; John 15:1-8*

Chapter 4

Protect and Sanctify Your Home

"When we speak God's Word into our home, we are raising the volume of spiritual authority over our home."

Home is Where the Heart is

Short, pithy expressions like "Home is where the heart is," "Home Sweet Home," and "Home is where you hang your hat" are all well-worn proverbs still handed down today because they contain some traditionally held truth. There is some speculation that "Home is where the heart is" came from the ancient Greek adage "Home is where the hearth is," but whether heart or hearth, we are definitely sentimental when it comes to thoughts of home. One friend put it this way: "If home is where the heart is, then my home is my parents' old house. I've never loved my own apartment the way I love their place." Most of us enjoy a good visit in someone else's home, but we look forward to returning to our own because, as another old saying goes, "There is no place like home."

It's fun to celebrate with others who are moving into a new home. Not long ago I enjoyed watching an old-favorite movie - *It's a Wonderful Life* - and was especially warmed by the scene in this Christmas classic where the Baileys go to welcome the Martini family into their new abode bearing gifts of bread, wine, and salt. The bread represented hope that the family would never go hungry, and the wine was a wish that joy and prosperity would always fill their home. Salt represented the "spice" that variety and change would bring to make life interesting.

One emerging housewarming tradition gaining favor is the House

Blessing. In this ceremony the new home is dedicated to the Lord during a gathering of family and friends. Often a pastor or priest is present, moving the group from room to room offering prayers for blessing and peace and anointing the doors and windows with oil for protection from evil.

In recent decades, home and family life have been the subject of many successful TV series and movies. People could project themselves, if only for a brief time, into one of the seemingly perfect families portrayed. Similarly, Thomas Kinkade became famous for creating unusual warmth in his paintings of quaint, softly- lit cottages that inspire people to imagine the happy life within and beckon them to step inside.

It's pleasant indeed when we can associate happiness and security with thoughts of home. Yet for many, the reality falls far short of the ideal. Even in the Christian community many homes are void of peace and stable relationships. Recently a friend shared that her granddaughter confided in her, "When Mommy and Daddy fight, I feel like I'm home all alone." "Home alone" can conjure up feelings of danger, harm, and even the risk of loss. Such children need far more than a security blanket to dispel their anxiety.

Do you ever feel that you are simply at the mercy of circumstances in *your* home? Are there behaviors or attitudes of family members or yourself that you would like to see changed? Most people would answer with a resounding "Yes!" How, then, can we protect and consecrate our homes?

Guarding Against Internal Intruders
If we could peel back the roof of every home and look inside, what might be revealed? In some places we would surely find a sweet, harmonious domestic life and observe the workings of strongly-knit relationships. In others we would, without a doubt, come upon scenes causing us to wonder what happened to the once hoped for peace and well-being of that household. Remember the little girl who felt "all alone" when Mommy and Daddy fought... Though we can't remove roofs and peer intently inside people's homes, we know from the things we see and hear, and from our own experi-

ence, that both kinds of home life exist and that most of us desire the peaceable one. God has given us spiritual authority and rights over our home, and it is time for us to exercise them (Genesis 1:27-28; Psalms 115:16).

Many of us wisely take care to protect our physical homes from external threats. We install alarms, sensor flood lights, dead bolts and window locks, and take other precautionary measures to guard against any dangerous intrusion. In the same way, it is crucial to put in place spiritual dead bolts to sanctify our homes on the inside and secure the spiritual well-being of our families. We cannot look the other way and ignore the fact that our homes are in danger of being trampled over by the powers of darkness. Our eyes must be wide open to the attacks, pressing us to stand against the flood of alcohol, drugs, immorality, and lusts of every kind that purpose to derail not only our youth but their parents and any other adult family member. Marital strife, divorce, and various forms of abuse are threatening to undo our families in no less measure than teen rebellion. It's time to discern between the holy and the unholy, the clean and the unclean, and to purify our own lives and homes. We turn that spiritual dead bolt every time we teach our children to honor and obey their parents and our young men and women to treasure God's commands and get wisdom that will be "life to their souls" and "cause them to find favor and high esteem in the eyes of God and man" (Proverbs 3:4; 4:22).

If the words and actions in our homes are contradicting God's growth in us, it may be time to invite Jesus to examine our thought life. The seeds of holiness and purity or derailment and destruction have much to do with the thoughts and attitudes that are cultivated in our homes. Certainly harmful attitudes can be as dangerous as any epidemic disease. One family doctor called in a pastor as a last-ditch effort to help a patient who, for unknown reasons, was dying. As the pastor listened to the patient's sad tale of how her husband had abandoned her for the good life with a new, younger bride, he was struck with how determined the angry woman was to not let her former spouse off the hook. In reality it was she who was on the hook, seriously ill from being held captive by the internal intruders of bitterness and un-forgiveness; her ruin was hardness of heart. Clearly, we cannot always control painful or disappointing life events that could defeat us, but what we can control is our response to them. Christ's indwelling presence in believers is always there to strengthen us when Satan attempts to gain a foothold in our heart (Philippians 4:13).

Ultimately, our greatest spiritual protector is Jesus who calls Himself a "Wall of Fire" around us and in our midst (Zechariah 2:5). He was the glory fire that protected Israel in her long wilderness journey and is that same separating, insulating fire for believers today. His presence is also with us to confront sin in our lives whenever we need His fire of refinement.

I went through an extended rough patch in my home with my son during most of his teenage years. There were times when it was all I could do to maintain my spiritual equilibrium. As much as I wanted easy answers, there were none. This made day to day, sometimes hour to hour, living with him an all-out challenge.

During those years I sought to maintain certain "constants" which seemed to act as divine protection for our little family of two, part of our "Wall of Fire," so to speak, because they were His wisdom for me. The first constant, or steadfast purpose, was for me to stand guard against spiritual attacks by praying God's Word. Not just reading it, but *praying* it for our protection and as a means of opposing a malicious enemy. "Be sober, be vigilant;" the apostle Peter warns, "because your adversary the devil walks about like a roaring lion, seeking whom he may devour" (1 Peter 5:8). A second constant was to hold firm in prayer for my son's future by praying God's promises for him. Thirdly, and most difficult of all, I resolved and worked to maintain peace in our home. Sometimes this meant letting go of a tough battle and literally leaving it in the Lord's hands. Maintaining peace with your teenager when your home is the battlefront can require the full use of your God-given resources, but deep inside I knew that a peaceful home had to triumph, even if the way of victory didn't always make sense or meet with the approval of others. Below is a summary, then, of the "constants" I encourage you to apply for the protection of your home:

- guard against spiritual attack by praying God's Word
- hold firm in praying God's promises for family members
- resolve to pursue and maintain peace in your home

I dare say that had I not been vigilant in implementing and maintaining these safeguards during my son's growing up years, I would have been subject to any number of internal intruders that temped me toward the ravages of uncontrolled anger, un-forgiveness, self-recrimination, regret....just to name a few. I will be eternally grateful for these guarding "constants" which the Lord, in His wisdom, imparted to me.

As I write this, the desired relationship with my son continues to progress and I can happily report that significant shifts have taken place within encouraging time spans. The battles have virtually ceased, and we actually have conversations we *enjoy*. I treasure regular hugs and the ease with which he now says - "I love you, Mom." And, needless to say, I'm ecstatic that my once homework-resistant, classroom-attendance opposer graduated from high school with honors! Indeed, there is no place too difficult for God to work.

One day recently I was reviewing with the Lord those long years of struggle with my son and wondering aloud if I should have taken different approaches to the problems we encountered. I questioned whether it would have helped if there had been a man present to overpower my son's high volume and considerable size, or if I would have been wiser sending him to a type of military school or one of those intervention camps for unruly teens. The Lord immediately impressed me that while I could have done those things and seen some outward improvement, my son would have returned home even more combative. He added that by my maintaining a spiritually peaceful home during the long storm, a tender place had been preserved and nurtured in my son, preparing a soft place for the Holy Spirit to land. It was great reassurance for me that the Lord had known all along precisely what my son needed and had guided me accordingly.

Raising the Volume of Spiritual Authority

Is the Word of God being read or spoken aloud in our homes? Is it a place where we pray aloud? **If walls could talk, what would they tell us?**

Paul told us in Romans that if we confess with our mouth that Jesus is Lord (specific spoken words) and believe in our heart that He has been raised (resurrected), then we will be saved (Romans 10:9). And in Genesis God spoke just a few well-placed and appointed-time words and voila! - the heavens and earth were created. "Now the earth was formless and empty, darkness was over the surface of the deep and the Spirit of God was hovering over the waters" (Genesis 1:2). Despite varying opinions on the origin of the universe, the Bible teaches that God effortlessly *spoke* creation into being. His mighty Spirit still hovers - over our homes, for example - ready to do amazing things. As we speak aloud His authoritative Words in our home, they act as lightning rods against the spiritual forces seeking to dominate and control (1 Peter 5:8).

By the creation account, we can see that there is something very powerful about God's Word being spoken aloud. We see *authority*. When we speak aloud God's Word and pray aloud to Him in our homes, we are raising the volume of spiritual authority there. Behind the physical space of a home, there is spiritual space, and it is up to us to assume the spiritual ruler-ship of our home whether we live alone or with others. Just like the *homesteading* principle mentioned in chapter two, we must take possession of what belongs to us in the spirit realm or it is guaranteed that the enemy will happily step in to seize it (John 10:10).

Not long ago I ran into some frustrations with my son over a particular issue. We had locked horns over a specific discussion a number of times, each of us standing firm in our position. After debating with myself about what action to take, I decided to stop talking to my son about it and start speaking with the Lord about the problem. He reminded me about His principle of speaking aloud His Word authoritatively into my home. It was an "aha" moment for me and I thought, "What took me so long?" I searched and found every scripture there is about honoring one's mother and father and then read them aloud in my home when my son was out of earshot (which is easy to do when his headphones are on). Down the halls and all around the house I spoke those Words! The next time I brought up the emotionally charged subject, I was relieved that we were able to talk it through and come to a resolution with which we both could live. I can only imagine how differently things might have been if I had understood and put into practice this nugget of wisdom at the front end of his teenage years!

Praising God aloud in your home is another very effective form of prayer and weapon of spiritual warfare. I thought I had a fairly good understanding of this until the Lord revealed to me recently that I wasn't honoring Him with all the praise He was due. This occurred one day when something quite positive had taken place for which I was praising Him. Suddenly my praise ended as I began to think about some concerns I had - even while happy about the victory just won. The Lord brought me up short and pointed out that *when I stopped the flow of praise, it stopped the flow of His Spirit back to me.* What a revelation! I had no idea such a thing was happening. In no way did I want to hinder the flow of His Spirit. In the days that followed, this principle continued to illumine my mind and alert me to even the smallest of ways I might be robbing Him of praise. Grateful for the revelation, I set about to re-map my thinking and responses and to replace them with thoughts and ways I knew He desired. Accordingly, I have been blessed by the changes both within and externally.

It didn't happen without practice, however. One night shortly after this revelation I had a fitful night of sleep. Instead of grumping around to myself about how tired I would be the next day, I focused on things I could praise God for: "Thank you, Lord, that I am warm. Thank you, Lord, that I know where my son is. Thank you, Lord, that I have all I need right here." And on it went for most of the night. When I jumped out of bed the next morning, I fully expected to be exhausted but was surprised to find that I was bright-eyed and bushy-tailed. Aha! I thought, "Praise is energizing and grumbling is depleting!"

One can keep adding dead bolts to the outside doors of their home with little effect on the inside intruders, or they can, with God's help, begin to strategically guard their home against, and in the face of, such unwanted entry. *The real truth is that "Home is where* **God's** *heart is; therein lies His authority"* (Luke 10:19). He is hovering over your home waiting to enter, but he will not do so uninvited. He is eager to gather the lambs in His arms and carry them close to His heart (Isaiah 40:11).

Leaving an Indelible Imprint

We are created in God's image, and He leaves His indelible imprint on us. Scripture tells us that God's Son radiates His glory and is the exact representation of His being, sustaining all things by His powerful word (author's paraphrase - Hebrews 1:2-3). God tells us that He even puts His law into our minds and writes it on the tablets of our hearts (Jeremiah 31:33).

Because God has written on the hearts of His people, I believe there is a deep desire within Christians to make a positive impact on the lives of their children and loved ones. A longing exists to leave an indelible imprint on them, an important legacy, if you will, of wise living according to Godly values and standards. It's not hard to identify with such a goal.

At times, however, people's plans and approaches to insure this go awry. Well-intentioned parents or persons of influence may, unwittingly, put on the wrong glasses or take up a mistaken road map and be swayed by mistaken priorities or leaning on their own understanding rather than seeking God's wisdom (Proverbs 3:5-6). They may have come under such worldly influences as wealth, status, or reputation and neglected to model things of eternal value. Imagine their perplexity when they see their children, or those they hope to inspire, focused on acquiring possessions or popularity, engaged in unhealthy competition, or inappropriately valuing good grades, performance, and pleasing others.

It can be tough to swim against the tide and learn new ways of thinking and doing. Personally, I often have to begin with what I call "re-mapping my thinking." Then I can begin to see and walk in God's ways and according to His goals. There is a *"Stairway to Heaven"* for every earthly challenge, a heavenly perspective awaiting our discovery. You could think of it like Jacob's Ladder that connected heaven and earth. Jacob "had a dream in which he saw a stairway resting on the earth, with its top reaching to heaven, and the angels of God were ascending and descending on it" (Genesis 28:12). God sent His angelic messenger to encourage this lonely traveler on his way to a new place. Like Jacob, we need encouragement to assess the spiritual condition of our homes and make needed changes. If we are going to spiritually "re-map" our homes, we will need to take a first step to "re-map" our thinking which is done by submitting areas of thinking and attitudes to the Lord for the transforming and renewing of our mind (Romans 12:2). In 2 Corinthians 10:5 Paul instructs us to "take every thought captive in obedience to Christ." "Re-mapping" our thinking and "spiritually re-mapping" our home really work together hand-in-hand. So what does that mean, and how do we go about it?

Spiritual Mapping

This "spiritual mapping" I have spoken of is a term used in the prayer community. It is a process used to determine certain spiritual realities, including the history of a certain geographic area, for the purposes of prayer, understanding, and strategic prayer warfare. We can apply this principle to our homes by conducting a spiritual mapping inventory to assess its current spiritual climate. This can easily be done with the participation of both parents or one parent. Likewise, a single person can take the inventory. Ideally, in the case of a two-parent home, the husband and wife would do this together, but the process is still powerfully applicable when only one of the parents is available.

The following are some questions to use as you get started. I am confident that as you pray about this process, the Lord will guide you toward an honest evaluation of your own situation. It can be quite helpful to have one or more close friends pray with you during the process.

Spiritual Mapping Inventory

Thoughtfully consider and write out the answers to the following questions:

1. What is the state of the different relationships within your home? What kind of words would you use to describe each relationship? For example: warm, friendly, loving, hostile, angry, unforgiving, conciliatory, gracious, impatient, tolerating, respectful, engaging, disrespectful, etc. If you are single, you can answer regarding the state of your relationship with the Lord.

2. What is the level of peace within your home? Are you personally at peace with yourself and God?

3. Describe the kind of communication in your home. Is the language uplifting and encouraging? Does it build confidence and goodwill? Does it erode self-esteem or crush the spirit? If you are single, answer these questions based on your self-talk (conversation with yourself) and things you say to God.

4. What are the priorities of your home? On what do family members focus their energy and time?

5. Is there honor and respect for others in your home? Do *you* honor and respect *yourself* as God does?

6. Is love displayed in your home? Describe in what ways that it is or is not. If single, are you receiving the love God has for you and loving Him in return?

7. Is God's Word being read in your home? How often? Is it ever spoken aloud?

8. Is prayer taking place in your home? How often? Is it being spoken aloud?

Spiritually Re-mapping Your Home
If your Spiritual Mapping Inventory reveals additional need for God's joy and peace, be encouraged! Things never have to stay the way they are! Now that you are aware of the spiritual condition of your home, you are empowered to do something about any area that needs change. By following the next steps you can spiritually re-map and strengthen your home through the transforming power of Jesus Christ. Every promise of God is your inheritance and the inheritance of your children (Psalm 16:6; 1 Peter 1:4; Matthew 25:34).

1. Acknowledge to the Lord the condition of your home and that

you are powerless to effect change on your own.

2. Review your answers to the inventory questions and ask the Lord to lead you to specific scriptures and Bible promises that apply to your situation. Engage a close friend or two to be praying with you. You may need to seek counsel from a Godly mentor or church leader to help you with Bible references. It is always wise to ask trusted Christians for help (Proverbs 24:6).

3. Pray aloud in your home using God's Word and promises.

4. Speak God's Word aloud in your home as a means of applying strategic spiritual warfare.

5. Pray Ephesians 6:10-17 for yourself and loved ones each day. "Put on the full armor of God so that you can take your stand against the devil's schemes. For our struggle is not against flesh and blood, but against the authorities, against the rulers, against the powers of this dark world and against the spiritual forces of evil in the heavenly realms" (verses 11-12). This spiritual armor consists of:

a. Belt of Truth

b. Breastplate of Righteousness

c. Boots of Peace

d. Shield of Faith

e. Helmet of Salvation

f. Sword of the Spirit

If you would like to gain more understanding about the armor of God and spiritual warfare, read *The Invisible War* by noted author and pastor, Chip Ingram.

Earlier we spoke of the importance of sanctifying our homes to secure their spiritual well-being. *Sanctify* means to *set apart for a sacred purpose.* What greater sacred purpose could there be than to lovingly defend our families as Christ loved the church? With God's help you can sanctify your home, bringing it under His full protection. Are you ready to raise the volume of spiritual authority in your home?

Do-Able Prayers for the Home

■ Lord, help me to speak your Word regularly into my home.

■ Lord, help me to pray aloud into my home.

■ Lord, help me find creative alternatives to keep your peace in the home.

■ Lord, help me to be steadfast in praying the armor of protection over myself and my loved ones.

■ Lord, help me to make the needed changes I learned from the Spiritual Mapping Inventory.

IN SUMMARY – Chapter 4

Home is where God's heart is. Jesus, as a "Wall of Fire," is our greatest spiritual protector (Zechariah 2:5). We can guard against internal intruders by spiritually re-mapping our homes and by raising the volume of spiritual authority through the spoken Word and prayer - all very do-able activities!

Key Verses: Genesis 1:27-28; Psalms 115:16; Luke 10:19

STUDY/DISCUSSION/REFLECTION QUESTIONS

1. Are you raising up an "altar of God" or an "altar of neglect" in your home? What could these terms mean?

2. Identify the extra safety measures described in this chapter for revitalizing the spiritual condition of your home.

3. How would you consider your role in the spiritual protection of your home? Are there any changes you could make to increase such protection?

4. If there are things currently compromising the peace of your home, what new approaches could you take to ensure that peace?

5. What does the author mean when she says there is a *"Stairway to Heaven"* for every earthly challenge, a heavenly perspective awaiting our discovery? How do you access that stairway?

6. What are the three "constants" that you can use to protect your home?

7. How would you go about re-mapping your thinking? When would you need to do that?

8. What are some Bible verses you could speak or pray aloud to address some of the challenges in your home's spiritual climate?

9. What are some verses you could declare in your home to claim your inheritance (God's promises)?

10. Take the Spiritual Mapping Inventory for your home. If you are meeting with a group for this study, it would be helpful to pray for one another as you do this and in susequent meetings to share how you have seen God at work during the process. One of the most encouraging and faith-building things we can do with others is to give testimony of how God is at work in our lives.

Pray for one another as indicated in #10, and pray the *Do-Able Prayers* in this chapter.

DIG DEEPER - Optional; refer to suggestions page

Ponder one of Jesus' names: "*...a sure foundation*" (Isaiah 28:16). God's promise through Isaiah in this verse assures us that no matter how uncertain our lives or the world scene may be, there is a solid rock on which we can stand. And that place is Jesus, our Sure Foundation. Consider how *He* is the solid ground for building your family and helping it to stand secure amid an instable culture.

These passages were referenced in this chapter: *Genesis 1:27-28; Psalms 115:16; Proverbs 3:4; 4:22; Philippians 4:13; Zechariah 2:5; 1 Peter 5:8; Romans 10:9; Genesis 1:2; 1 Peter 5:8; John 10:10; Luke 10:19; Isaiah 40:11; Hebrews 1:2-3; Jeremiah 31:33; Proverbs 3:5-6; Genesis 28:12; Romans 12:2; 2 Corinthians 10:5; Psalm 16:6; 1 Peter 1:4; Matthew25:34; Proverbs 24:6; Ephesians 6:10-17*

Chapter 5

Turning Your Thoughts Into Prayers
Prayers on the Go for Work and School

*"Every one of your connection points is a potential
wireless spiritual 'hot spot' for the Kingdom of God."*

How we use our time is important, but for most of us a big part of our waking hours are already committed. Typically we work - whether inside or outside the home - or we attend school. The complex social and cultural conditions and physical demands in these environments can cause Christians to wonder what their workplace or school might be like if transformed by the power of Jesus Christ. Does it excite you to imagine heading out each morning in anticipation of what God is going to do? If so, and you long for such change, then this chapter is for you!

How influential are you in your corner of the world? It's well-known in the business realm that one of the key qualifiers for high level positions and promotions has to do with a person's ability to successfully influence others for the betterment of the organization. Having recruited for large corporations for many years, I can tell you that we always had a keen eye out for those with that special ability to positively affect people and situations around them. Managers with this skill will be particularly adept at teambuilding and forming positive alliances within an organization. When a teacher displays this kind of charisma, students will go out of their way to line up for their course. Not everyone excels in such skills, but those who do are highly prized and sought after.

Creating Spiritual "Hot Spots"

Did you know that in God's eyes *you* are highly prized and sought after (Psalm 139:13; Jeremiah 1:5)? With or without the recognition of others, God has already counted you as worthy to be a person of great Kingdom influence. You have been courted and recruited by the King Himself, selected as the only person who will connect with a certain circle of people and events in the precise way and time He has arranged. Thus, you are in the unique position of being able to influence the spiritual climate in all the intersections of your life. No other person has your exact set of connection points in life, and each of them is an opportunity to affect another person or situation, a potential wireless spiritual *hot spot,* for His Kingdom.

Try to imagine the potentiality of all believers activating prayer at their particular connection points. A Holy unseen network (the Holy Spirit) begins to send powerful signals into those connections in your domain. Even random encounters become opportunities to reach the lost. Chance meetings, unexpected openings in conversations, unplanned acts of kindness become spiritual *hot spots* with the potential for birthing new believers, new life into dead relationships, new hope after failure... Envision countless such associations coming alive in explosions of faith and lighting up the world for Jesus!

The potential is present for this kind of Holy Spirit outpouring to occur everywhere as believers are praying and birthing spiritual *hot spots* around the world. Even the hardest of hearts can be softened as they have a front row seat to changed lives and healed relationships (John 14:12)!

Following are two examples where Kingdom *hot spotting* happened that resulted in an explosion of God activity.

Two male co-workers – one a manager of the other – were pondering together a very difficult personal situation one of the men was going through. Though neither was a Christian, they decided to look to the Bible for answers and ended up reading it all through the night. After ten hours of reading and discussing, both men decided to accept Jesus as their Lord and Savior. When morning arrived they came upon the passage about becoming baptized and determined then and there that since God said it, they would do it! So they got up and set out in search of a church in which they could be baptized. They made several attempts, but for one reason or another every church they approached was either unable or unwilling to help them. After a night of caffeinated drinks and being high on Jesus, one can only imagine how they must have looked to those they approached. But these men were not easily discouraged. Once again they asked the Lord to direct them to a church that would baptize them. They hopped in the car and one of them soon saw what he described as an unusual light source and gave instructions to the driver to move in that direction. Wild-eyed, determined and scared, they followed the light and found themselves at the doorstep of my pastor who welcomed them inside, heard their story, and promptly called together everyone on campus that day to witness this beautiful event. Thankfully, I was arriving for an appointment with my pastor at that very time and was blessed to become part of this wonderful ceremony and to hear the amazing testimony of these two young men. And if that weren't cause enough for celebration, we all learned that the office manager of our church was the mother of one of the young men and had been praying for her son for many years. Even more astounding, the son had not known that this was the very church where his mother worked!

The second example of Kingdom *hot spotting* took place very recently. A friend of mine suffered the experience of a devastating house fire in the middle of the night in which she and her husband barely escaped with their lives. Shortly after, during a visit to their counselor, it was suggested that they find some time away from the home where they were staying in order to talk and process together the many events that were suddenly taking place in their lives. He recommended a little "hole in the wall" restaurant near his office. Upon leaving the appointment, my friend and her husband momentarily forgot about the suggestion and went off in another direction. But eventually they remembered and turned back to find the little restaurant and enjoy a quiet time together. When the waitress brought the bill, a gentleman sitting nearby got up and came over to say he wanted to pay for their lunch. Then he simply told them to pass the blessing on. But my surprised friend began to wonder why the offer had been made and after a few minutes approached the generous man. "Can I ask you a question?" she inquired. He nodded. "Was there something that stirred in you to want to do this for us?" she asked. "I like to bless people," he replied. And again he said, "Just pass the blessing on." At this, my friend's husband began telling the gentleman that their house had just burned down. The man was silent for a moment and then spoke these words: "I am a pastor and have been praying for days for help in finishing my sermon... which is about *fire*. Please, tell me more."

While the pastor and husband were speaking, my friend heard a nearby woman crying and approached her to see if she could be of help. The woman, seated with her husband, tearfully explained that she had overheard the conversations, was a Christian herself and was overwhelmed by witnessing God at work in such a powerful way. In talking together, my friend and the couple delighted in discovering a number of common connections. The wife was a Financial Counselor and promptly made her services available to my friend and her husband. The woman's husband worked in assisting college students in locating funds. Upon hearing that my friend's son was having some difficulty with college expenses, he immediately offered his help in finding the money needed for his schooling. In describing the scene of these noonday encounters, my friend laughs and says, "It was like having church in the restaurant!" One can only wonder how many other patrons and workers were affected by their eye-witness of God in action in that little restaurant.

To the casual observer it may seem as if these events were simply random - no rhyme, reason, or source behind their occurrence, but we know better! There was a God-activity convergence at the right time and place because people were praying at their points of connection. This was not spiritual "spontaneous combustion." Rather, an already present Source for the activity was at work in response to the prayers of God's people. In fact, in the first example it is quite likely that prayers had been offered up on behalf of these two gentlemen at their place of business by Christian colleagues, or even others who may have adopted their company in prayer in addition to the prayers of one faithful mother. In the second example there may have been others in the little cafe - preceding these events - who prayed for God's presence in this place of business. Imagine others who may have asked God to touch the patrons and staff while giving thanks for their meal. The pastor had been praying for divine connections and was clearly living out a praying life with his actions towards my friend and her husband. How wonderfully God blessed him back with the inspiration for the end of his sermon that would now go on to bless many others. And so it occurs with opportunities wherever we go.

Now I want to tell you about four amazing men of God who are in the spiritual *hot spotting* business. If asked, all would be quick to say they are not doing anything special. As I got to know them over time, I noticed one unique characteristic they shared in common. They each humbly brought their apportioned fish and loaves (their measure of faith) to a weekly Bible study in service to the Father. No fanfare, no applause, just a hunger to be part of what God is doing. I came to know them and be part of their on-going Bible study at their place of business in one of my seasons of tent-making when I did some consulting for a high-tech firm in Silicon Valley. This study was mostly attended by engineers and leaders in the company. They had been meeting to study God's Word and pray for quite a number of years. Though their group had not grown much over the years and attendance by many of the members was sporadic, there was a faithful remnant of four that regularly came together in faith for what God would do. They have not seen a harvest with their earthly eyes yet, but I am convinced that what they are doing is spiritually *hot spotting* into this organization. One day (if it hasn't already happened), their prayers and God's presence will converge into a hotbed of spiritual activity for someone else in that company, maybe even similar to the example of the two men who both had an explosion of faith that I just described. In the meantime, the Lord calls these four "faithful!" "A cord of three strands is not quickly broken" we are told by the author in Ecclesiastes (Ecclesiastes 4:12)! I believe the Lord has formed them into a *four strand cord* for just such a time as this.

They continue to meet, they continue to pray, they continue in faith

(Hebrews 11:1). These four brothers are virtual "prayer-mobiles" as they prayerfully walk the corridors of their business as well as praying across continents during business travel. Additionally they have partnered with me as part of my prayer team and in ministry support, thus furthering their borders of ministry and influence in the spiritual realm. They may tell you there is nothing special they are doing, but the fact is that by staying the course and meeting together for prayer, Bible study, and support on a weekly basis, they are quite literally throwing a *spiritual lifeline* to those around them. Just picture for a moment what it would look like if our earthly eyes could see into the spirit realm. Multiple *spiritual lifelines* dangling from heaven within reach of all God's children. Some are there for comfort, some for rest, some for hope, some for shelter in a storm, some for salvation, etc. What a sight to behold! That's exactly what happens when we pray at our connection points; our prayers add additional *spiritual lifelines*. These four Godly men are dropping *spiritual lifelines* into their connections as they pray, thus making an eternal difference in the spiritual realm.

There are many of you, like this faithful remnant of four, who have been faithfully meeting and praying in a variety of locations, longing to see a harvest with your earthly eyes. Don't give up! Be encouraged, indeed, for Jesus tells us that "whoever can be trusted with very little can also be trusted with much" (Luke 16:10). Be bold, be strong, for the Lord your God is with you (Joshua 1:9)! Keep bringing your apportioned fishes and loaves to the service of the Father and let Him multiply them for you. That is the business that Jesus is in! He has given you a measure of faith and welcomes your offering (however small it may seem to you) with thanksgiving in His heart (1 Corinthians 12:9).

Every day Christians can be moving further in this direction, adding more and more spiritual lifelines across the world as they mount up with wings as eagles and spread their prayers across the land. Momentum will be gained as increasing numbers of believers find their voice in prayer and exercise it at their unique set of connection points.

Turning Your Thoughts Into Prayers

So how do we go about turning ordinary connections into spiritual *hot spots*? One surefire way is... *by turning your thoughts into prayers* (2 Corinthians 10:5).

Prayer is do-able both in the workplace and school. It need not be complex or lengthy. It can happen in the morning as you carry on little conversations with God while getting ready and thinking about the day ahead. Even as you drive, your thoughts can become prayer targets as you mull over certain challenges in front of you. Maybe you can identify with some of the following examples:

■ You are thinking about a problem that has to be solved and find yourself praying, "Lord, I need your help in this perplexing situation, and I'm all out of ideas."

■ You are thinking about a colleague or classmate with whom you are experiencing difficulty. "Lord," you begin to pray, "please step into my communications with Joe; give me wisdom in both my inward reactions and my outward replies."

■ You are realizing that *you* can be difficult at times, so your prayer becomes, "Lord, help me to overcome my tendency to be competitive, as rivalry never brings the best outcome."

Turning your thoughts into prayers creates wireless spiritual *hot spots* where none had previously existed. A helpful way to understand this is to compare it to the experience we all have with cell phone coverage. You know how frustrating it is when speaking with someone and you enter a "dead zone" or get a dropped call. No amount of fiddling with the phone will activate the signal until you come into the proximity and signal of the next cell tower. It's not so different in activating your wireless spiritual *hot spot.* Each time you pray at one of your connection points, you activate a signal that others can plug into, whereas just moments before it was a virtual dead zone with heaven-bound communications non-existent. Unlike cell towers that are fixed in location, thus limiting where and when the connection takes place, each of us has the opportunity to spark into existence new Kingdom *hot spots* with our prayers at our natural connection points.

Hmm, I wonder what it is like for the Lord when He comes into a spiritual "dead zone" with us- a broken connection? Perhaps the loss of contact comes just when He is about to tell us something. But we have surged off to do the next great thing in life, all the while continuing to guard those places that we want to keep hidden from Him. Thankfully He does not give up on us. Recalling Jesus' words from chapter 3 instructing us to abide in Him- "I am the vine; you are the branches," (John 15:4,5)- we know how vital it is to maintain a steadfast connection to Him, for without Him, we cannot bear fruit. In fact, apart from Him, we can do nothing. *Surely our relationship with the Lord is the most vital spiritual hot spot possible.* Through this essential unity with Jesus, we will not only produce much fruit for His Kingdom but will experience His joy, His unfailing love and His matchless presence in our lives. Andrew Murray, a prolific Christian author (1828-1917) marveled, "How wonderful the lesson of the Vine, giving its very life to its branches! All depends on having your life full of God and His power."

My friend Susie lives a branch-like life of abiding in Christ. Her prayers are an exercise of her union with Him. She tells of a time when she was annoyed with a co-worker who made much ado over the mundane task of mail delivery. Every day this woman would come rushing down the halls commanding everyone to stop and pay attention to the mail she was delivering. Susie's annoyance with this co-worker grew to the point where she began to plan being away from her desk at mail delivery times or *whenever* the woman was likely to come by. One day Susie realized the absurdity of her behavior and decided to turn her thoughts into a prayer, which also became a form of taking her thoughts captive to the Lord (2 Corinthians 10:5). "Lord," she said, "I am sorry for my attitude and want to thank you for Jean who obviously cares a great deal about my mail. In fact, I'm grateful that she cares so much about my mail that I never need to worry about it at all. So thank you, Lord, for this woman in my life."

With this simple prayer revealing her attitude and approach to an everyday concern, Susie allowed Jesus to light up His Kingdom *hot spot* within her while at the same time creating a *hot spot* for Jean (Philippians 4:8). We may never know this side of heaven the impact Susie's prayer had for Jean, but we do know that the prayer allowed Susie to get out of the way so that God was free to work in Jean's life and in her own.

There are infinite ways to produce these spiritual *hot spot* connections in your workplace or school environment. I know of people who leave early for their day at work or school in order to walk their building or campus, silently praying for peace, blessings, salvation and protection as they tread that land. In the prayer community this is called "Prayer Walking." These walkers report that while walking and praying, they often will receive a strong impression to intercede for a particular person or for something specific.

Another example of spiritual *hot-spotting* occurs when we speak God's Word into situations as the Holy Spirit directs. There is life in His Word by which people are born again, cleansed, healed, and set free. Arm yourself with scripture at some of your connection points and see some new things established (Psalm 119:11). Declare some seeds of salvation, some freedom seeds, some seeds of unity. Why not pray God's Word for your co-worker's broken heart - "Lord, You are the One who *heals the brokenhearted and binds up their wounds*" (Psalm 147:3)? Pray God's Word for some of those people in your sphere of influence and look for the harvest it can produce. Paul encourages us in 1 Thessalonians 5:16-19, to rejoice, pray continually, give thanks and do not quench the Holy Spirit.

One company I worked for was preparing to move to a new building. A God-thought came to me to print up scripture verses which a friend and I literally dropped into the walls of the new building during construction as we prayed for the company. This was another means of spiritual connection in the workplace.

Undercover Prayer

Recently Alaska Airlines announced that they were discontinuing the use of their prayer cards on their meal trays. In the early 1960's a process began to eliminate School Prayer from the U.S. public education system by slowly changing the meaning of the First Amendment through a number of court cases over several decades. Aren't you glad that you are a *Child of the King?* It's a brilliant strategy on the part of our Father. As such we do not need to obtain the permission of an airline company or school or our government in order to pray.

The beauty of prayer is that it can go where man cannot and be completely undercover! You may not have direct interactions with the CEO of your company, the school principal, or the Chancellor, but by prayer you can give rise to many wireless spiritual *hot spots* which are able to become birthing grounds for God's activity - sometimes in places where your presence and His presence might otherwise not be welcome.

You can do this "undercover prayer" as you walk to meetings or classes or pray silently for individuals in hallways or in elevators. You can become a virtual prayer-mobile! In one workplace, I observed that people were strangely silent in the elevators, so I decided to try a little experiment. On my way to work I began praying for the people whom I would see in the elevators that day:

"Lord, soften their hearts…"
"Lord, open up pathways of communication for me."
"Lord, give them a good day at work."
"Lord, help them with a work challenge they are facing today."

I also made sure to greet each person warmly and wish them a pleasant day. Over time, the elevator atmosphere changed dramatically. Even people's countenances were altered as smiles and greetings began to be exchanged regularly. Clearly, *it does not take a lot of time or effort to make changes in the spiritual climate in your sphere of influence.*

Lighting up a Dark Place

When I was hired into my first position in the high-tech world I had prayed in advance that the Lord would send me to a place where I was needed. The job was an administrative role supporting one of the directors in the company. On my very first day of work I was struck with the impropriety of my environment. To my dismay, I discovered that my cubicle was right between two chain-smoking, cursing employees. Pornography around the company was rampant. It wasn't long before I was complaining to the Lord that He must have made a mistake in sending me to this place! Obviously it was beyond help, and I was clearly in no position to influence change. He promptly reminded me of my request to be sent to a place where I was needed and assured me that He knew what He was doing. A deep peace that was definitely not of this world came over me, and I settled in for the long haul (Philippians 4:7). My days were mostly filled with running errands around the company, so I began to pray silently wherever I went - short prayers... *Do-able* prayers...

"Lord, help this man."
"Lord, bless this team."
"Lord, I pray that good words would be spoken instead of cursing."
"Lord, may people know there is something different about me."
"Lord, I ask that your presence will go with me wherever I go."

After three months, I felt prompted to make an appointment with the company's President. My ears seemed to hear the Lord saying, "This is the way; walk in it" (Isaiah 30:21). One day I ran into him in the hallway and, with fear and trepidation, asked if I could meet with him. This was completely nerve-wracking to me as I had no idea what I was supposed to see him *about*! As our meeting time approached, I sensed the Lord saying; "Trust me. You will know what to say" (Mark 13:11). While I was a bit nervous, I found myself telling the company President about some of my experiences working in personnel-related areas in the private sector and made known my desire to work in Human Resources should there ever be an opportunity. He was cordial and friendly but made no promises.

When another three months had passed, the President called me in to inform me that the Human Resources Manager was no longer with the company and to ask if I would like to step into the role. I was stunned! But pleased. What I later learned was that at the time of the meeting with the President three months earlier, the company was in the process of making some decisions about the future of this position. My appointment with him had been in God's perfect timing! Amazingly, and by God's grace, the culture began to shift and within eighteen months of my arrival all smoking and pornography had been eliminated. The company had raised its standards and become a professional environment.

I was hired into a job in which I had no earthly influence, but I prayed as if I had the influence of the King at my disposal - because I did! As I regularly turned my thoughts into prayers, the Lord saw fit to give me a position through which I could bring His influence right into the heart of the firm. For the years I worked there, I was a respected and integral part of the inner workings of that company.

God has deliberately designed us to connect with our surroundings. We are to prayerfully involve ourselves in the lives of others and in situations and events in our sphere of living. The most exciting connections occur when the Christ life in a believer sparks a new *hot spot* whereby God's activity is set ablaze into the very culture of an organization or school or into the life of another whose soul is awakened to God's hope and everlasting life. I value the words of well-known Bible teacher, author, and psychologist, Dr. Larry Crabb: "When we pour into another even a little of the life that, at the cost of Jesus' death, has been poured into us, connection happens." May God help us to pour ourselves out in time, prayer, kindnesses, affirmations...bringing to our connections the Light of the World. If we live for Christ, *we* are lights that reflect Him and point others to Him. Matthew encourages us: "You are the light of the world....Let your light so shine before men, that they may see your good works and glorify your Father in heaven" (Matthew 5:14-16).

Do-Able Praying on the Go

Dropping *spiritual lifelines* from heaven through prayer is extremely do-able! This is especially so in the case of high performers and over-achievers. Over the years I have both observed and heard high-ranking male and female Christian business and ministry leaders lament over their hectic schedules. Some of these folks even refer to themselves as being in the "attention deficit disorder" category as they dash from one task to another or pace about as if they are walking off unrestrained energy. This kind of praying is especially well suited for these folks who are constantly on-the-go, but it is equally well-suited for the rest of the population. Next time you're off and running, inquire of the Lord; "Lord show me today who needs a *spiritual lifeline* of... ."

... joy
... faith
... hope
... peace
... praise
... refuge
... wisdom
... healing
... courage
... comfort
... salvation
... forgiveness
... confidence in Christ

... then drop that prayer into your connection point as you are on the go and watch God work!

Verses related to the spiritual lifelines; Psalm 28:7; Hebrews 11:1; Psalm 119:74; Proverbs 3:5-6; Philippians 4:7; Psalm 139:14; Psalm 91:2; James 1:5; Psalm 107:19-21; Deuteronomy 31:6; 2 Corinthians 1:3-5; Mark 10:27; Isaiah 40:31; Psalm 103:8-12; Psalm 147:3; Psalm 91:1; Hebrews 13:8

IN SUMMARY – Chapter 5

Each of us is a designer creation by God. No one is exactly like us or will have the same connections with others that we have. By turning our thoughts into prayers, we can transform our connection points into spiritual *hot spots* of God's activity wherever we go in the natural intersections of life. We can move about freely in prayer as virtual "prayer-mobiles" because we have the influence of our King at our disposal 24/7.

Key Verses: 1 Thessalonians 5:16-19; 2 Corinthians 10:5; Philippians 4:8-9; Matthew 5:14-16

STUDY/DISCUSSION/REFLECTION QUESTIONS

1. Is there a particular connection point in your life-sphere that is being transformed into a spiritual *hot spot*? If so, what kind of prayers for others could help you bring Him honor and glory in this connection?

2. What do you think it means to pray as if you have the influence of the King at your disposal?

3. What challenges are you currently facing at work or school right now that would benefit from prayer?

4. How can you turn your thoughts into prayers for those challenges?

5. What are some do-able ways you can pray for your workplace, colleagues, or classmates?

6. Have you ever witnessed a "spiritual hotbed of activity" as described in this chapter's two examples? If so, share your experience with the group.

7. Discuss ways in which you can envision spiritual *hot spotting* taking place more frequently.

8. Can you imagine an inspired outcome to your prayers? What would it be?

9. What is a *spiritual lifeline*? How does it work? How can you be part of giving it?

Have fun with the *spiritual lifeline* list under the "Do-able Praying on the Go" section. Choose a different one each day of the week and ask the Lord to show you where to drop that prayer. Start by praying in your small group asking the Lord to show you how and where to pray.

DIG DEEPER - Optional; refer to suggestions page

Search for some particular Words (verses of scripture) to pray for people at your connection points who need salvation, healing, hope. Or think of the connection you have with a particular city. What scripture could you declare in prayer over that place?

These passages were referenced in this chapter: *Psalm 139:13; Jeremiah 1:5; John 14:12; Ecclesiastes 4:12; Hebrews 11:1; Luke 16:10; Joshua 1:9; 1 Corinthians 12:9; 2 Corinthians 10:5; John 15:4,5; Philippians 4:8; Psalm 119:11; Psalm 147:3; 1 Thessalonians 5:16-19; Philippians 4:7; Isaiah 30:21; Mark 13:11; Matthew 5:14-16; Psalm 28:7; Hebrews 11:1; Psalm 119:74; Proverbs 3:5-6; Philippians 4:7; Psalm 139:14; Psalm 91:2; James 1:5; Psalm 107:19-21; Deuteronomy 31:6; 2 Corinthians 1:3-5; Mark 10:27; Isaiah 40:31; Psalm 103:8-12; Psalm 147:3; Psalm 91:1; Hebrews 13:8*

Chapter 6

Fortifying the Wall of Prayer in Your Church

*"The enemy has assumed a neighborly posture and
ignores our no trespassing signs."*

Fences are friendly, walls are formidable. Walls mean business. They are structures that keep intruders out. Neighborhood fences, however, often have knotholes in them, you can see over the top, and because there is shared ownership, a relationship dynamic is present. But walls are a different story altogether. Their structure conveys a "Keep out - you have no business here" kind of message. Walls imply there is something very important on the other side, something worth the time and expense to guard.

Some of us have been praying for a long time and yet it may seem like our prayers are building friendly fences instead of impenetrable walls to guard our homes, our churches, and even our cities and nation from attack. In the spiritual realm, *the enemy has assumed a neighborly posture and ignores our no trespassing signs.* He peers in, slithers under, peeks over and battles us constantly over our property line. He doesn't believe us when we tell him he is not welcome. He strategically deploys intruders of the worst kind: deception, discouragement, doubt, and defeat.

These intruders are one reason why prayer is easily defeated for so many Christians. Prayer is at the top of Satan's hit list. If the enemy can silence one voice at a time, and often enough, he will gain much ground in rendering the Church powerless or severely crippling her in carrying out her mission. We must not allow our adversary to silence our prayers because, as he well knows, a praying life is the *fire-power* for every believer and the Church, which will one day be presented to the Lord as "a radiant church, without stain or wrinkle or any other blemish, but holy and blameless" (Ephesians 5:27). Pastor Chip Ingram captures this truth well when he says in his book *The Invisible War,* "Power falls where prayer prevails."

I don't know about you, but I am ready to say, "ENOUGH!" If your question is, "What can we do to fortify the *Wall of Prayer* for our church," I'm glad you asked...

Intercessors, Prayer Warriors, and Watchmen

In this chapter I have made a number of references to the people I call Intercessors, Prayer Warriors, and Watchmen. As you might guess, generally speaking these folks belong to what I have earlier called the *Five Percent* group. Though I often use the terms interchangeably, the following are some differences which, in their simplest form and from my own observations, characterize the three groups:

Intercessors: Those who are often called to intercede for the needs of others and for specific situations. Even though every believer is called to pray, Intercessors have a special passion to do so.

Prayer Warriors: A pit bull comes to mind when I think of a Prayer Warrior. Once this person receives a prayer assignment from the Lord, he/she is unwilling to "let go" or cease praying, until the Lord releases them. The assignment can be of long or short duration.

Watchmen: These people of prayer generally carry broader assignments from the Lord involving prayer for church leaders, the Church at large, and for territories, cities, and the nations.

Though a *Five Percenter* is usually more dominant in one of these three areas - Intercessor, Prayer Warrior, or Watchman - it isn't uncommon to see, for example, an Intercessor seriously praying for their nation or a Watchman praying with the intensity and duration of a Prayer Warrior. Mine is a limited treatment of this subject, but you can read more about the roles of Intercessors, Prayer Warriors, and Watchmen by exploring other resources on the "Featured Prayer Resources" page.

Rebuilding the *Wall of Prayer*

In Chapter One I introduced the idea for rebuilding the *Wall of Prayer* when mentioning that I was eight years into prayer ministry leadership before I learned anything about prayer walls, let alone those that were in disrepair. As you may recall, the initial inspiration came to me as I was reading the Book of Nehemiah which is said to be a blend of prayer and action. The broken down wall of Jerusalem and its rebuilding is the heart of this book. God had stirred and gripped Nehemiah on behalf of his people in Jerusalem, and through a variety of divinely inspired steps, guided him to return to that city to rebuild its walls.

When God provided for me a mental image of the *Wall of Prayer* in disrepair, I was stirred in my heart and gripped for action on behalf of my people, the church. The picture of each man, woman, and child picking up their prayer stone with the accompanying message that the wall could not be rebuilt by pastors and Intercessors alone had moved me deeply, creating in me a passion to help people find their voice in prayer and become a partner in rebuilding the *Prayer Wall*. Now, eight years later in my prayer leadership role, I have had a lot of time to pray, study and reflect on this *Wall of Prayer* and how it works within the context of our churches. Among some of the questions I have asked myself and God were:

■ How is the wall rebuilt?
■ What is each person's part?

In the scene that had unfolded before me years earlier, I was struck by certain observations. One was that the men, women, and children were not lugging, trudging, or having any difficulty in lifting and carrying their individual prayer stones. Each was picking up a stone that appeared to be perfectly sized and suited for them. The translation for me was that God has given each person in His church a role of prayer that is a perfect "fit" for them.

Next I saw the Intercessors, Prayer Warriors, and Watchmen literally marching atop the *Prayer Wall* patrolling and keeping a spiritual watch (praying) for the church, each with their own assignment. These people are often referred to in the prayer community as the Watchmen. They are appointed and stationed on top of the wall for the spiritual good of the church (Jeremiah 6:17). Obviously the wall was wide enough to hold them, but what about its height and strength? Is there anything the rest of us can do to impact that, I wondered? Indeed, do we have a part at all in how high and strong that wall can become as a defense against a powerful and determined enemy?

The Modern Day Watchman
Who are the modern day Watchmen and how do they function? We can draw some helpful insights from particular passages in the Old Testament. In many churches today there are mature, trained and trusted Watchmen who are known and who function for the church in one or more of the following ways:
- are of solid reputation, known as having an "ear to hear" (Isaiah 52:8)
- their spiritual antenna are engaged (Song of Songs 3:3)
- are trusted and called upon to give a word in season (Isaiah 21:11-12)
- are willing to obey the Lord's instruction even at personal risk (2 Kings 9:17-29)
- have earned the ear of the pastor/leaders (2 Samuel 18:24-25)
- communicate potential spiritual threats to pastors/leaders (2 Samuel 13:34; Ezekiel 33:2-3)
- are on-call for around the clock prayer, often being awakened in the night (Isaiah 62:6-7)
- are strategically positioned for the thick of a spiritual battle (Jeremiah 51:11-12)
- are often messengers of expectancy and hope (Psalm 130:5-6)

When looking at this list of Watchman characteristics, I am amazed at the breadth of their ministry calling and what they bring to the church. You might even be asking yourself, *"If God has designed people to be Intercessors, Prayer Warriors, and Watchmen, then why does the church need **my** prayers?"* That is a good question. For its answer, let's look at some wall building principles from the Book of Nehemiah to understand how the wall of Jerusalem came together.

Wall Building Principles from Nehemiah

The building or repairing of *Prayer Walls* is key to the security and protection of the church and to her peace, order, and effectiveness. Such was the case for the restoring of Jerusalem's wall in Nehemiah's time. There is much we can learn about the work of building *Prayer Walls* by examining the following truths from the Book of Nehemiah.

1. *Prayer is for everyone.* Nehemiah didn't take on rebuilding the wall around Jerusalem by himself. He enlisted all the people. The priests began the work and then came the merchants, the farmers and gate-keepers, and even the perfume-makers. In the same way, every man, woman and child needs to find their voice in prayer and take their place on its wall. The work belongs to all believers. Every person in the Body of Christ is destined to be a wall worker for the Lord (see Nehemiah 3). In John 15, Jesus told His disciples that he had "appointed" them to bear fruit. The word means "strategically placed them." He put each one in the place where He wanted them to be.

2. *Pray corporately in unity.* In Nehemiah's day the people not only worked, they worked *together* - side by side to close the gaps in the wall in the face of opposition. Many times in the Book of Nehemiah you see the phrase "next to him worked..." this person or that, repairing a part of the wall or one of the gates in the wall. It is the same for God's people today. Each of us is to take up our assignment and work hand-in-hand with God and side-by-side in prayer with fellow believers to close any breaches through which the enemy could gain entry to weaken the church. And like the wall workers in Jerusalem, we too will face opposition and find ourselves subject to the adversary's attacks and intimidation. Since Satan is a destroyer and not a builder, his efforts will focus on bringing about disunity, strife, and ill-will toward a brother or sister in Christ - in short, anything that can divide God's people and stop the work. Nehemiah 4:7-8 gives us a list of the Jews' enemies who, when they heard that the walls of Jerusalem were being restored and the gaps were beginning to be closed, "became very angry, and all of them conspired together to come and attack Jerusalem and create confusion." However, as the people prayed to God and set a watch against them day and night,

they were able to stand united and firmly press through the opposition. As we apply these principles today, we will see the gaps in the *Prayer Wall* close and press through our opposition.

3. *Pray relentlessly.* With a sword in one hand and a brick in the other, Nehemiah's wall workers stayed at the task round-the-clock. In other words, someone was always on the job. In the same way, as each of us carry out our prayer assignment from the Lord, there will be the needed prayer coverage because of His timing and supervision (Nehemiah 4:23).

4. *Leaders must pray.* Just as Nehemiah, God's appointed leader, devoted himself to work on the wall, the participation of church leadership in wall building activity is crucial in seeing a strong fortress of prayer emerge. In order to motivate, encourage, and unify the workers, Nehemiah had to identify himself with the need. Likewise, the support and involvement of church leaders is vital to the rebuilding of the *Wall of Prayer* (Nehemiah 5:16).

5. *Pray at the Gateways.* Jerusalem's burned gates also needed to be reconstructed by Nehemiah and his workers. In fact, the gates were important structures within the wall itself . They were not only points of entry but were symbolic of the life within. Trade, legal decisions, and basic social interaction took place at these openings in the wall. Today, some of the significant points of entry into the church and opportunities to participate in its life are through the pastoral and support staff, worship leaders, and through youth, children's, and various outreach ministries. Prayer is greatly needed to generate new life and fellowship through these modern-day gateways in our churches.

Weak or Fortified Prayer Walls?
What do *Walls of Prayer* look like in the church today? To help us understand this better, we can look at two types of prayer walls:

Weak Prayer Walls - A weak *Wall of Prayer* is a low wall with open gaps due to little prayer in the church. The enemy can easily scale and slither through such walls and begin his work of demolition. The following are typical signs and symptoms of a church with *weak prayer walls:*

- loss of members
- financial problems
- a focus on problems
- disunity; in-fighting
- gossip and finger-pointing
- growth largely by transfer and births
- problem-solving first; prayer a last resort
- exhaustion, burn-out of staff and volunteers
- high turnover of staff, leaders, and volunteers
- endless meetings concerning endless problems
- efforts to please man's wishes for programs and decisions rather than seeking God's desires for such

Fortified Prayer Wall - A fortified *Wall of Prayer* is a high wall due to continuous and sustained prayer by a church community. Such prayer results in the wall's breaches being repaired and the gaps being closed, thus prohibiting the enemy from having easy access. **A church where every person finds their voice in prayer will find its' wall being as high as is needed for that church.**
The following are traits of a church with *fortified prayer walls:*

- unity (Psalm 133:1)
- esteeming of one another more highly than oneself (Philippians 2:3)
- faith and anticipation of God's enabling to overcome problems (Ephesians 3:20-21)
- blessing and speaking well of one another (Ephesians 4:2)
- strong financial stewardship (2 Corinthians 8:1-3; Luke 6:38)
- ability to bless those who move on from the church (Galatians 6:10)
- productive meetings that include testimonies of God's faithfulness (Lamentations 3:21-24; Hebrews 11)
- the sights and sounds of new believers and ministries (Acts 2:41, 12:24)
- healthy balance of work and relaxation for staff and volunteers (Ecclesiastes 3:1)
- longevity of staff, leaders, and volunteers who invest in the Kingdom (Ephesians 4:13)
- prayer as a first resort (Philippians 4:6-7)

■ seeks to find the mind of Christ for all decisions (1 Corinthians 2:16)

Having seen some of the results of both weak and fortified prayer walls, it is also helpful for the Body of Christ to understand the effects each kind of prayer wall has on the Watchmen and Prayer Warriors who have been stationed by the Lord's assignment to keep watch or guard their church in prayer.

In the case of a church with *fortified prayer walls*, the Watchmen and Prayer Warriors will be energized for their assignments. They are nourished and will thrive in an atmosphere where they have a strong prayer foundation on which to stand. A fortified prayer wall assists these prayer servants to see off into the distance spiritually and recognize potential threats that can be averted through prayer and warning to the leadership.

Unlike the Watchmen and Prayer Warriors serving in a church with *fortified prayer walls*, those who are keeping watch in a church with weak prayer walls are subject to exhaustion and burn-out. One of the reasons for this is that they will naturally step in to make up for the prayer deficit while at the same time attending to their usual prayer guarding of the church, a work that often involves intense spiritual warfare. Pulling double duty will, in time, undermine their strength and stamina. Such stress cannot be sustained indefinitely without deep discouragement setting in, sometimes followed by withdrawal from their prayer role or even from the church altogether.

With weak, low prayer walls, is it any wonder that the church in America is in crisis? It is observed by many of us who work in Prayer Ministry that the average duration of a prayer leader's service in a church is 6-18 months. Not only are the prayer leaders leaving, many pulpits sit empty for lack of a pastor.

CNN Reports 9/27/2011

Church attendance across the country dropping. A new decade-long survey (2000 – 2010) of American congregation's shows religious health and vitality are weaker than they were 10 years ago.

David Kinnaman
38-year-old president of the Barna Group, an evangelical research firm, is the latest to sound the alarm. In his new book, You Lost Me: Why Young Christians Are Leaving Church and Rethinking Faith, he says that "Eighteen to twenty nine year-olds have fallen down a black hole of church attendance" and that "there is a 43 percent drop in Christian church attendance between the teen and early adult years."

Focus on the Family Reports:
1,500 pastors in America leave the ministry monthly.
7,000 churches in America close their doors each year.

The church is in a spiritual battle and needs all resources available so that we can *present the Bride, God's Church, as Holy and blameless in the day of Christ Jesus* (Ephesians 5:27). Rebuilding the *Wall of Prayer* is as important today for the protection and mission of the church as was the rebuilding in Nehemiah's day of Jerusalem's wall. As God's appointed one, Nehemiah has provided us a successful model for rebuilding by breaking down the job into bite-size, do-able tasks that were suited to the individuals and families as they worked side-by-side to make it happen. Some carried bricks, others spread mortar, some designed gates....We can use the same approach to rebuild the *Wall of Prayer* in our churches today as we are all fellow citizens and members of one body (Ephesians 2:19-22; Colossians 3:14-16).

The power and effectiveness of corporate prayer cannot be underestimated. As Deuteronomy 32:30 explains: if one can put a thousand enemies to flight, and two can put ten thousand enemies to flight, just imagine what we can do to the plans of our adversary when two or more of us come together in prayer. "If two of you agree about anything you ask for, it will be done for you by my Father in heaven" (Matthew 18:19-20).

An Example of Fortifying the *Wall of Prayer* in One Church
Some years ago our church found out just how effective this bite-size, do-able kind of prayer could be. We were in transition with our future Senior Pastor finishing up his seminary degree before taking

the helm of the church. He was still working in the role of Music Pastor during the transition while also shouldering the responsibilities of seminary work, family, and being mentored by the outgoing Senior Pastor. We had been through a very rocky time as a church, and it seemed that the enemy was intent on continuing his attacks on every side. One day in prayer the Holy Spirit nudged me that it was mission critical to mobilize daily continuous prayer coverage for our new pastor and his family for the remaining nine months until he was officially installed. More than forty people joined with me to provide this daily, persistent prayer. We divided up the days and hours and rotated the schedule in a way that worked for us and put together some specific prayers to carry forward. As Prayer Leader, I checked in frequently by e-mail with everyone, and each was faithful in their praying to the end. Oh what a grand celebration we had at our pastor's installation! It was no ordinary celebration, for it also marked the culmination of our partnership in prayer with the Lord over the preceding months. Many of the people wrote out prayers and words of encouragement which were collected into a book for our new pastor. He has commented many times since then on how important our prayers during those nine months were for him and his family and how often those prayers and blessings have served as ongoing encouragement for him.

Praying in one accord over a period of time was a new experience for many of the people who participated. It drew us closer as a Body of Christ, building unity and faith as we witnessed the Lord work in some marvelous ways while we labored side-by-side in prayer.

You can be part of fortifying the *Wall of Prayer* in *your* church, and following are some examples of how you can go about it:

Do-Able Prayer for Fortifying the *Wall of Prayer* in Your Church
■ Pray for the Prayer Leader or coordinator in your church; reach out and ask how you can support him/her.
■ If there is no Prayer Leader for your church, pray for one.
■ Pray for your pastor and family without fail. Determine specific areas where prayer is needed. Pray for courage and strength, for protection of their time with both the Lord and their family, and for an abundance of grace in their life (1 Peter 5:1-4).

■ Pray for the entire staff of your church. Coordinate an effort to divide the names to be prayed for (Hebrews 13:17).

■ Pray for the gateways of your church - the significant entry points such as support staff, worship leaders, youth and children's workers and outreach ministries. Identify and give special attention to these (Nehemiah 3).

■ Pray for the next generation to develop an authentic, growing faith in Jesus Christ (Deuteronomy 6:5-7).

■ Pray for one another, both in person and privately (James 5:16).

■ Pray for the church leadership. Besides pastors, most churches have leader positions such as elders and deacons. Pray that their spiritual lives will be worthy of their calling (Ephesians 4:1).

■ Pray for the teachers in your church to handle the Word of God rightly and to meditate in His Word (2 Timothy 2:15; Psalm 1:2).

■ Pray for the church services, the worship and praise times, for the Word of God to be proclaimed with boldness, and for the Holy Spirit to prevail (Psalm 98:4-9; Hebrews 4:12).

■ Pray the Pew. Take a moment to pray for the people in your pew on a Sunday morning. Ask God to meet them personally and to insure that their life will count for Jesus (2 Corinthians 1:3-11). Our church has created "Pray the Pew" cards and placed them in the hymnal racks. E-mail me to request our example.

■ Pray the prayers from *Do-Able Prayer* for abiding, protecting, and blessing others in the traffic of life.

Just imagine with me for a moment what might happen in our churches if. . .

■ we prayed on our drive to church, seeking the Lord's mind and heart for our body of believers?

■ we all arrived five minutes early to pray in the sanctuary?

■ we each prayed for the person sitting next to us?

■ we asked Jesus how we might participate in what He wants to accomplish during the worship and fellowship times?

As each of us takes our place in prayer for the church, we will begin to put in place impenetrable walls that guard and keep our churches from harm. Won't you join me in helping to build a high, fortified *Wall of Prayer* in your church? When the enemy is hard pressed to find any gaps through which he can enter, your church community will be strengthened and better shielded from Satan's onslaught for the Kingdom work at hand.

Let's close all the gaps in the *Wall of Prayer*, leaving no breaches. May it be so, Lord! May it be so!

IN SUMMARY – chapter 6

A praying life is the *fire-power* for every believer and the church. God has given each person in His church a role of prayer that is perfectly sized for them. As each of us takes our place in prayer, we will begin to put in place impenetrable *Prayer Walls* that guard and keep our churches from harm instead of building friendly fences with poorly protected boundary lines against the enemy. The right amount of *fire-power* will release the church to her true mission and destiny.

Key Verses: Ephesians 2:19-22, Colossians 3:14-16, Ephesians 5:27

STUDY/DISCUSSION/REFLECTION QUESTIONS

1. Do you see your church as having friendly fences or impenetrable walls? Elaborate.

2. Based on this chapter, how fortified do you believe the *Wall of Prayer* is around your church? Elaborate.

3. How do you understand the importance of your prayers for the church?

4. What are some ways you will begin to pray for *your* church?

5. Has the idea of taking your place in prayer for your church been a new discovery for you? If so, in what way?

6. What do you think the following statement means? "The extent to which the Intercessors, Prayer Warriors, and Watchmen can be fully effective for the church is directly proportionate to how fortified the *Wall of Prayer* is."

7. Why is prayer for your pastor so important?

8. What does it mean that there is a role of prayer in the church that is sized just right for you?

9. Identify and list what you believe were the benefits for the church and the pastor when the people were mobilized to pray for the pastor in the example given in the section titled **An Example of Fortifying the *Wall of Prayer* in One Church.**

Pray together using the list of *Do-Able Prayers* for Fortifying the *Wall of Prayer* in your church.

DIG DEEPER - Optional; refer to suggestions page

Study Nehemiah 1:1-11 and describe the progress of Nehemiah's prayer:

- What Nehemiah did before he prayed...
- How he described God...
- Who he prayed for...
- What confession he made...

These passages were referenced in this chapter: *Ephesians 5:27; Jeremiah 6:17; Isaiah 52:8; Song of Songs 3:3; Isaiah 21:11-12; 2 Kings 9:17-29; 2 Samuel 18:24-25; 2 Samuel 13:34; Ezekiel 33:2-3; Isaiah 62:6-7; Jeremiah 51:11-12; Psalm 130:5-6; Nehemiah 3; John 15; Nehemiah 4:7-8; Nehemiah 4:23; Nehemiah 5:16; Psalm 133:1; Philippians 2:3; Ephesians 3:20-21; Ephesians 4:2; 2 Corinthians 8:1-3; Luke 6:38; Galatians 6:38; Lamentations 3:21-24; Hebrews 11; Acts 2:41, 12:24; Ecclesiastes 3:1; Ephesians 4:13; Philippians 4:6-7; 1 Corinthians 2:16; Ephesians 2:19-22; Colossians 3:14-16; Deuteronomy 32:30; Matthew 18:19-20; 1 Peter 5:1-4; Hebrews 13:17; Deuteronomy 6:5-7; James 5:16; Ephesians 4:1; 2 Timothy 2:15; Psalm 1:2; Psalm 98:4-9; Hebrews 4:12; 2 Corinthians 1:3-11; Colossians 3:14-16*

Chapter 7

The Gift of a Spoken Blessing

"God began the world with a Spoken Blessing and Jesus closed His earthly ministry with a Spoken Blessing."

Does the hair on your neck rise when you hear four-letter words or angry condemning words that are the cause of someone's personal anguish? Are there words you would like to eliminate from the vocabulary of your teenager? Or does your spirit feel grieved when people close to you get carried away with intense conversations that erupt into heated arguments?

Most of us can relate in some way to the above questions and would likely answer "yes" because we know from history and our own experience that words have amazing power to destroy or to bless (James 3:3-6). How well we know their ability to build up or tear down such values as integrity, truth, and respect, not to mention people and nations.

Looking a little more closely at the significance of words, the Bible says they actually reveal what our heart is like - "...out of the overflow of the heart the mouth speaks" (Matthew 12:34b). And James 3:2 indicates that our words are so powerful that their control determines self-control in every other area of our life. Perhaps most important of all, our every word and thought are known and examined by God Himself. Think how differently we might choose our words knowing that God is listening, not only to our spoken words, but to our heart.

God's emphasis on the importance of what comes out of our mouth can further be seen in His first act after creating Adam and Eve - He blessed them (Genesis 5:2)! Centuries later we read of Jesus giving a *spoken blessing* to His disciples as His last act on earth before His Ascension (Luke 24:50-51). *God began the world with a **spoken blessing** and Jesus closed his earthly ministry with a **spoken blessing**.* The power and untold benefit of words that bless should not be underestimated, the results being for the edification (building up) of His people (1 Thessalonians 5:11).

Surely, then, there is power in the words we speak to change the course of conversations and relationship dynamics, such as the ones described at the beginning of this chapter. I believe that an especially effective way of doing this is by bestowing words of encouragement and *spoken blessings,* even when we are limited to speaking or praying blessings silently. In fact, I found in my research that "praying" and "blessing" are words often used interchangeably. I am inclined to agree that there is not a strong line of division. It has been said also that a blessing is a hopeful prayer, a way of asking for God's favor to rest upon others. So whether we are blessing a friend or praying for a complete stranger, an important meeting, or a family vacation, we are copying Jesus' way as He walked this earth and as He intercedes for us now with blessing while seated at the right hand of God.

Bestowing a blessing is a universal rite, an act practiced throughout the world and thus able to affect the whole world. God's Word urges us to bless not only friends and loved ones but our enemies as well (1 Peter 3:8-9). As mentioned before, words have the power to promote good or evil, to build up or to destroy. The purpose of blessing is to confer abundant, heavenly life upon someone or something. Remember the House Blessing ceremony mentioned earlier in this book where prayers were offered for the well-being, peace, and prosperity of a family? When we bestow a blessing, we are acknowledging God in His rightful place as the Lord and ruler of the earth, the One with all the power to bring about the blessings. He, in fact, is the One *most* worthy of our blessing, for He has blessed us by forgiving our sins, healing our diseases, crowning us with love and compassion, and satisfying our desires (Psalm 103:3-5).

While it's inspiring to think of sincerely imparting words of encouragement and blessing, it isn't as easy as one might think. Remember the Scripture, "...out of the abundance of the heart the mouth speaks" (Matthew 12:34)? These words of Jesus tell us that what we say reveals what is in our heart. In Biblical language the heart is the center of one's spirit, from which spring our emotions, thoughts, motivations, and ultimately our actions. When we have difficulty blessing or praying for others, it is wise to look within and find out what is "going on inside." The psalmist David wasn't sure he could accomplish this - being honest with oneself isn't easy - so he invited the Lord to divinely examine his heart, to test his thoughts and motives and then refine and purify them (Psalm 26:2). God's probing exam is the most thorough, but we can begin to look within by frequently checking and becoming aware of our self-talk.

Self-Talk and Flash Points

I was stunned recently to read that psychologists believe we talk to ourselves up to 50,000 times a day! With some training these internal conversations with ourselves can be positively uplifting. The success of many athletes-in-training, in fact, is due to intentional positive self-talk. Our sense of well-being and ability to enjoy life stems largely from our thoughts. Proverbs 23:7 says this about man: "...as he thinks in his heart, so is he."

But there is another side wherein people inflict on themselves a barrage of negative self-talk ranging from doubts and complaints to bitter criticism of self and others. It can be helpful to tie this negative self-talk to the scientific concept of a "flash point" and ultimately to our words that can either dishearten and afflict or encourage and bless. Wikipedia say this: *The **flash point** of a volatile material is the lowest temperature at which it can vaporize to form an ignitable mixture in air. Measuring a flash point requires an ignition source. At the flash point, the vapor may cease to burn when the **source of ignition** is removed."*

To better understand how a flash point is connected to our self-talk just think of how one itty bitty harshly spoken word or action can bring you to an emotional flash point resulting in an explosion of anger, defensiveness, or worse. The trigger may not even be a deliberate offense, yet you *perceive* it to be and respond disproportionately to what is said or done. Just moments before, the sun was shining in your corner of the world, but a brief interaction now has your head spinning with negative thoughts that are quickly multiplying, amplifying, and dragging you to the pit. What draws us into such places of defeat? I believe the Lord has shown me that whether we are the recipient of a planned attack or some misinterpreted event that causes us anguish, our flash point reaction is often tied to the aforementioned negative self-talk.

It shouldn't be surprising, then, that one of Satan's primary and most effective tactics is to get in on our self-talk by delivering an onslaught of negative, self-defeating thoughts that become sources of ignition for behaviors that not only damage ourselves but can harm our relationships. But do we have to be his victim and allow our minds to be filled with thoughts that are opposed to Truth and God's plans for us? No, and the key to victory is found in Romans 12:2: "...do not be conformed to this world, but be transformed by the renewing of your mind..." Just how does such a metamorphosis as *mind renewal* come about? Scripture indicates that the change comes by the work of the Holy Spirit as believers study and meditate on God's Word that reminds us of who we are in Christ, how much we are loved by Him, and of His constant presence with us (2 Corinthians 5:17; John 3:16; Philippians 1:6; John 14:18). As our minds are renewed, we will be better prepared to stop, or at least slow the *burn,* in trying situations. We may not always be able to control our feelings, but we can control our thoughts that so greatly affect our feelings and behavior. 2 Corinthians 10:5 teaches that we are to "...bring every thought into captivity to the obedience of Christ..." Imagine how our disciplined thinking, empowered by our indwelling Holy Spirit, could affect not only our ideas and motives but our desires and decisions.

This past year I wrote a skit for one of our prayer conferences called *The Diary of a Colt.* This humorous little sketch was a first-person (more accurately a first-*animal*) account of the self-talk of the donkey colt who carried Jesus into Jerusalem on the day we celebrate as Palm Sunday. There was knee-slapping laughter as the skit was performed because people could so personally relate to the "goings on" inside the head of the doubtful young donkey as he is selected and then begins his mission. I invite you to have a peek at the little colt's self-talk. . .

Excerpts from *The Diary of a Colt*

Though my owner was agreeable to let me go to Jerusalem when the disciples came to get me, I did not feel so agreeable. I wanted more information. For example, what kind of business did they want me for anyway? And how long would I be gone? How did they know if I even wanted to go with them? They were strangers after all. Couldn't they see that I was comfortable having no demands upon me? My schedule was my own, and I was happy where I was. But what could I do? So I went with them...reluctantly.

The strangers quickly led me to their destination. Finally we reached a clearing where I saw Jesus surrounded by a small crowd. "Oh no," I thought, "what's this all about?" Suddenly some garments were thrown on my back. "Hey, watch it!" I wanted to shout. I had never had anything on my back before, and I wasn't at all sure I liked it. But before I could protest, Jesus was also sitting on my back. I felt scared... Could I bolt and run, I wondered? Hardly! Not with this load I was carrying. Whoa! I wondered if Jesus knew what I was thinking. Maybe when He sent these strangers to town to fetch me, they had gotten the wrong address. I had never been ridden before. This was indeed a first. I felt a little wobbly and weak and wasn't sure that I could properly carry Jesus, but I would do my best. The road was dusty and the crowd was growing and gathering momentum as we moved along. There were moments when the people were pressing up so hard against us that I thought we would both collapse under the pressure. They were clamoring and yelling all kinds of things.

I began to question whether it was a mistake to let Jesus ride on my back. After all, Jesus wasn't popular with everyone. Would I be criticized too? Would anyone ever want to use me again? This could ruin my reputation with the townspeople! My owner might even decide to sell me after he heard what I had done. And what would happen to me then? A new location, a new owner - oh no!

I was getting tired and sweaty from the journey, not to mention my wearying thoughts. "How much longer?" I groaned to myself. I was growing increasingly impatient with the conditions and chaos around us. Why should anyone have to put up with this? Let alone a little colt without any experience. They should have chosen a better qualified donkey and one who was stronger. No one told me how long this journey was going to take or when it would be over or what the outcome would be...

Then, in a flash, everything changed for me! We had slowed to a stop at a point where the crowds were so thick we couldn't move. Slowly, ever so slowly, I turned my head and looked up just in time to lock eyes with Jesus. His deep, penetrating gaze stopped me in my tracks. Time stood still. His eyes were glowing with love, filled with warmth, and exuding patience and tenderness. This connection with Jesus was more powerful than anything I could ever have imagined. My impatience, stubbornness, doubt, and grumbling simply melted away. I wanted nothing more than to serve Him with my every breath. How grateful I was that He had chosen me for this journey and not given up on me when I was wobbly, weak, and grumbling.

In this comical little skit we can see that much of the colt's self-talk was negative and unproductive - just as such thinking can be for us. What was the turning point for him? He stopped just long enough to turn his eyes upon Jesus. It was nothing within himself that made the difference. Similarly, when we turn our eyes upon Jesus by sitting in His presence and taking in His Word, our internal conflicts will begin to melt away and His truth will set us free (John 8:32).

As we are able to turn our negative flash point words into *spoken blessings* and words of encouragement, we become to someone else what Jesus was to the colt in the story. We can carry His presence right into an opportune encounter, breathing new life into the thought life of another. We might even call it a *positive flash point* for the recipient.

We have already said that *mind renewal* comes by seeking the mind of Christ through scripture, prayer, and disciplining our thoughts to the obedience of Christ. The following are a few examples of bringing our thoughts into captivity and changing our self-talk:

Scripture - "Therefore, if anyone is in Christ, the new creation has come: the old has gone, the new is here" (2 Corinthians 5:17).

Renewed **Self-talk -** "I am a new person in Christ. The old is gone and the new is here. I 'm no longer captive to old defeating behaviors and attitudes."

Scripture - "I can do all this through Him who gives me strength" (Philippians 4:13).

Renewed **Self-talk -** "Nothing is impossible. With Christ I can tackle and accomplish anything. I'm convinced that God can make a way right now where there seems to be no way."

Scripture - "...being confident of this, that He who began a good work in you will carry it on to completion until the day of Christ Jesus" (Philippians 1:6).

Renewed **Self-talk -** Even though I am feeling depressed right now about my life I am going to recognize that this is a temporary feeling and the Lord wants to replace my thoughts with His thoughts. I am going to trade those thoughts for God's promise to me that He is present to work out everything in my life and bring it to completion in His way and in His time.

The way to life and renewed self-talk is the way of God's Word. "How can a young person stay on the path of purity? By living according to your word. I seek you with all my heart; do not let me stray from your commands. I have hidden (treasured) your word in my heart that I might not sin against you" (Psalm 119:9-11). When we arm ourselves with positive, Scripturally-based self-talk, we are far better prepared to impart *spoken blessings* and words of encouragement to others along the way.

Miracle in Sweden

In 2008 a divinely-led, life-altering experience brought me to a deeper understanding of the power of a spoken blessing in a way I had never known. This occurrence took me thousands of miles from my home in California to my grandparents' homeland of Sweden. However, this was not the original plan. There was the possibility of a little sightseeing in Sweden close to the Danish border, but outside of that I had not given any serious thought to travel into Sweden. My purpose was simply to visit a close friend and her family in Roskilde, Denmark (or so I thought). Airline tickets had already been purchased for my fifteen year old son and myself to make the journey in June. Imagine, then, my surprise when one Friday night in March I began to sense a very strong prompting from the Lord to find my grandfather's family in Sweden. This seemed to me an utter impossibility, yet I believed it was the Lord stirring me to action. And so it was that I submitted to His urging and asked for His help.

My maternal grandfather had died many years before, and since my mother had also been gone for a number of years, I had no one to ask about our Swedish heritage. The story that had been passed down was that my grandfather had arrived in America as a young man but subsequently lost all contact with his far away family. We didn't know why the relationship with his family had ended, except that he had indicated their disappointment in his not sending them money from America.

Not sure where to begin, I pulled down a box containing old photos and scribbled on notes left by my mother. To my surprise I came across a torn yellowed piece of paper listing the names of my grandfather's eight siblings. At least, I thought, this was a start. And though I wasn't particularly adept at navigating internet search engines, I relentlessly plugged words in until I came across a site where I found other people looking for lost family members in Sweden.

Adding my name and the few details I knew to the website, I pleaded for anyone with any information to please contact me as I was planning a trip in June and hoping to locate in advance any living relatives.   I quickly discovered that all birth and death records at the time of my grandfather's birth were kept in the churches. One

needed to know the name of the Swedish parish where their rela-
tive lived in order to conduct any serious historical family research.
Until the latter 1900's the parish housed the vital statistics, or otherwise known as "household examination rolls" of every family
member. This, in addition to the need for being able to speak and
read Swedish! It all seemed like the impossible dream.

To my complete astonishment, however, within 24 hours of my
post I received two unrelated e-mails in reply to my query. The first
was from a gentleman in Sweden and the other from a man in West
Virginia. Both were hobbyists who were moved by my appeal for
help in locating my grandfather's family. I do not exaggerate in
telling you that within five days these two men-angels provided me
with enough information that I could even track two generations *beyond* my grandfather! Further, the information gathered by each
man was corroborated by the other and by the scant information
my mother had put together in a family tree album. On top of that,
birth and death records and correct family names were all provided
to me free of charge. Needless to say, I was overwhelmed with gratitude for this miracle that all took place at lightning speed!

Within one week I was on the phone with two relatives who be-
longed to the family line of my grandfather's brother. Fortunately, in
one case, it was an eighteen year old young man who spoke very
good English. We scanned pictures back and forth and were equally
amazed at the resemblance of the family members. Within a short
time one of the relatives invited us to stay with their family. Thus
my son and I, my friend Hanne from Denmark, and her daughter
Emily all traveled to Sweden for five remarkable days in the sum-
mer of 2008. To my surprise, my cousin had arranged a family reunion of about thirty plus relatives from around Sweden to greet us.
Some of them had not seen each other in thirty-five years. We were
warmly welcomed with balloons and a sumptuous Swedish feast.
The joy of being reunited seemed to flood every heart.

During our visits we were able to piece together and solve many of
the mysteries that had surrounded the one hundred year old separation in our family. The living relatives in Sweden were from an
older brother of my grandfather. These kin actually knew very few

details about other family members. Amazingly, they were not even aware of the existence of the last five of my great grandfather's children; they only knew of the first four of the nine children. It was only from the information I provided that they learned about the other relatives. And to think that I was hoping to learn from *them*! They were thrilled to have more knowledge of their roots but also quite surprised that I had been able to obtain this information when living so far away. Certainly it had surprised me too, however I knew that this entire journey with all its revelations had the fingerprints of the Lord all over it.

We discovered through records that my grandfather's father had been a poor dirt farmer living in a part of Sweden where farming was very difficult work. We also learned from death records provided to me that my grandfather's mother died at an early age when the last two children were very young. In our discussion times, we relatives thought it likely that, following her death, the younger five children would have been scattered among other relatives or neighbors who could care for them. In that day the condition of the family probably caused its members a lot of shame. This and the probable separations could explain why the living relatives in Sweden knew nothing about that chapter of my great grandfather's life.

Ship records reveal that my grandfather, at the age of sixteen, became a crewman on ships that traveled abroad. It was on one such voyage, after a few years of this work, that the tide of his life would take a dramatic turn and provide the opportunity for him to seize a long held dream. A vessel he was working on was shipwrecked off the coast of Africa, making it necessary for the crew to be picked up by a ship whose next stop was America. My grandfather recognized his opportunity, jumped ship, and entered the U.S. without any papers. Thus he was never an official immigrant through Ellis Island. But the appeal of making a new life in America would have been strong for a young man essentially orphaned at a young age and knowing all too well the rigors of trying to eke out a living on unforgiving farm land back in Sweden. So he chose America, eventually moving to Nebraska where he met and married a young Swedish girl named Esther. August and Esther would have six children and relocate to Turlock, California. My mother was one of those six children.

I was especially grateful for my Danish friend Hanne who helped with translation by being able to speak both Swedish and English. Through her efforts I began to perceive that my Swedish relatives felt a strong, sad disconnect with their past because of the secrecy and separation within the family as they grew up. Somehow the sorrow of their loss brought me to the realization that it had really been the same for us who lived in America. Not wanting to relive the sadness of his early life in Sweden, my grandfather rarely spoke of those years. I can just imagine my mother sitting him down in his later years and, with her persistent questions, prying out of him the names of his siblings. Over the years I could sense a kind of emotional undertow in our family, an unspoken awareness of loss that clearly affected the family dynamic on this side of the ocean.

A growing momentum in my spirit began to take place during the family reunion, an impression that something important was about to happen. There was a sureness in my heart that the Lord had divinely directed me to Sweden at this point in time and for a particular purpose. I found myself in a state of excitement and anticipation.

Finally there came a moment when I was propelled into action. Without knowing exactly why, I felt impressed to gather the heads of the families. Then, with Hanne's help, I explained to them my desire to extend a *spoken blessing* and prayer for all the family, thanking God for ending the 100 year old separation between us. All were agreeable and without hesitation joined hands as I began to speak and pray. I could literally feel something pop in the spiritual atmosphere during those moments. Separation, darkness, shame, and isolation came into the healing light of Jesus that day. Even a vast ocean could no longer keep us apart, for God had now connected us through the pronouncement of His strategic blessing over our family. The visible joy of release that followed was indescribable and uncontainable!

That same freedom would carry over to America and be experienced during the next family reunion of cousins here. The undertow described earlier, that downward pull I had always felt at family gatherings, was now replaced with a new ease and joy in being together. I felt assured then that the family wound had been healed. What an unexpected bonus! In its place something new had exploded into life on both sides of the ocean. In my mind it became a *Kingdom Flash Point* - a positive flash point or ignition of connectedness and hope.

Initially I had thought the purpose of my trip across the pond was to enjoy a mother-son vacation while visiting a dear friend in Denmark. But God had a far greater plan. His intention was living proof of Ephesians 3:21 which describes our God as one "...who is able to do immeasurably more than all we ask or imagine..." His matchless plan would remove the long-standing divide in a family and include a *spoken blessing* powerful enough to release its members to a future of new relationships with one another.

Opportunities for Spoken Blessings

We live in a time of worldwide demolition. Daily we witness the destruction of values... truth...peace...relationships. We have torn down integrity and purity. Yet there are alternatives to the wholesale tearing down process. We can - and must - do something about building up people and affecting situations in our corner of the world. Not just building up other believers, but deliberately seeking to bless those who do not even know Christ. Through our words of life and grace, they may seek Him and find Him, for He delights to reveal Himself to others as He did to us.

All around us are opportunities to offer prayers or give *spoken blessings* and words of encouragement. We live in a hurting world where countless people seldom, if ever, find themselves on the receiving end of words that heal or inspire with courage and promote peace. We can be messengers for them to experience first-hand God's loving-kindness in their life. Our prayers become blessings and our blessings become prayers. An example of a prayer-blessing often used by pastors at the end of a church service is the Aaronic blessing from Numbers 6:24-26 (see below). This blessing was essentially a prayer asking for God's divine favor and protection, His mercy and compassion, and His approval and peace upon the one receiving it. You could memorize the entire blessing, or excerpts from it, and find yourself surprised at the opportunities to use it:

Numbers 6:24-26
24 The LORD bless you and keep you;
25 the LORD make his face shine on you and be gracious to you;
26 the LORD turn his face toward you and give you peace."

Or you might consider:
Psalm 121:5-8
5 The LORD watches over you - the LORD is your shade at your right hand;
6 the sun will not harm you by day, nor the moon by night.
7 The LORD will keep you from all harm - he will watch over your life;
8 the LORD will watch over your coming and going both now and forevermore.

People weigh our words. Comforting or offensive, full of grace or grudging, words often stick in our hearts and become part of our self-talk. Imagine for a moment what could happen if words of blessing and encouragement began to outnumber the words of cursing and discouragement that fill our world. You can speed the process of change by offering prayers and *spoken blessings* to your family members and those around you. It may seem like a small investment on your part, but huge rewards await you - blessings in return such as I experienced with my family on both sides of the ocean. We can all be part of outnumbering destructive flash points and promoting those *Kingdom flash points* that bring forth life and spark hope.

I have provided a collection of scripturally-based blessings from the Psalms that reflect love, caring, and encouragement which you might find yourself using to warm hearts and brighten the days of people with whom you cross paths in life. Some of these blessings could easily be shortened. For example, look at the first one. You might say to someone in parting "May the Lord show you the wonder of His great love today," or "May the Lord keep you as the apple of His eye."

Scripturally-based Blessings

■ May the Lord show you the wonder of His great love and keep you as the apple of His eye (Psalm 17:7-8).

■ May the Lord teach you His way and lead you in a straight path (Psalm27:11).

■ May the Lord bless you with abundant provisions (Psalm 132:15).

■ May your mouth be filled with laughter and your tongue with songs of joy (Psalm 126:2).

■ May the Lord give you the desires of your heart and make all your plans succeed (Psalm 20:4).

■ May the Lord counsel you and watch over you (Psalm 32:8).

■ May the Lord give you refuge in the shadow of His wings (Psalm 57:1)

■ May you pass a legacy of praise to the next generation (Psalm 79:13)

■ May God hear the cry of your heart (Psalm 38:12).

■ May God strengthen your heart during this time (Psalm 73:26).

Other blessings to try on for size. . .

■ "I bless you, son/daughter/husband/wife/friend as you go about your day."

■ "I leave peace and blessings on your home."

■ Thank you, God, for my home; I pray a blessing over it today."

■ "May the Lord bless you in your new position."

■ "May the blessing of joy be within you and the blessing of love flow from you."

■ "God bless you."

IN SUMMARY – Chapter 7

The fact that God began the world with a spoken blessing and Jesus closed His earthly ministry with one, underscores for us the power and benefits of words that bless. These two acts of *spoken blessings* are well appointed bookends in-time, containing an irrefutable God in display. The baton of blessing has been passed to His children to speak forth His creative blessings into a world hungry for Him.

Key Verses: 1 Thessalonians 5:11; 1 Peter 3:8-9; Matthew 12:34B; James 3:5

STUDY/DISCUSSION/REFLECTION QUESTIONS

1. How do the "In Summary" comments impact you?

2. Do you ever experience negative or defeating " flash points?" Elaborate or journal your thoughts about this.

3. What is a main way we can decrease negative self-talk?

4. Who is the source of condemning thoughts?

5. What is the answer for addressing such thoughts?

6. Do you recall giving a *spoken blessing* to someone? Elaborate.

7. What might be *your* biggest challenge in giving a *spoken blessing*?

8. What do you imagine our world would be like if words of blessing and encouragement began to outnumber the words of cursing and discouragement that fill our world? What do you think would be different?

9. As a small group exercise; brainstorm together and record 40 ideas for giving *spoken blessings* and practice giving them over the next 40 days.

Practice some of these blessings on one another.

DIG DEEPER - Optional; refer to suggestions page

These passages were referenced in this chapter: *James 3:3-6; Matthew 12:34b; James 3:2; Genesis 5:2; Luke 24:50-51;1 Thessalonians 5:11; 1 Peter 3:8-9; Psalm 103:3-5; Psalm 26:2; Proverbs 23:7; Romans 12:2; 2 Corinthians 5:17; John 3:16; Philippians 1:6; John 14:18; 2 Corinthians 10:5; John 8:32; 2 Corinthians 5:17; Philippians 4:13; Philippians 1:6; Psalm 119:9-11; Ephesians 3:21; Numbers 6:24-26; Psalm 121:5-8; Psalm 17:7-8; Psalm27:11; Psalm 132:15; Psalm 126:2; Psalm 20:4; Psalm 32:8; Psalm 57:1; Psalm 79:13; Psalm 38:12; Psalm 73:26; James 3:5*

Chapter 8

God's Heart For the Nations

*"From one man he made every nation of men,
that they should inhabit the whole earth; and
he determined the times set for them and the exact
places where they should live" (Acts 17:26).*

Should we concern ourselves with praying for people and places far away? Surely there are people in their own country praying for them. Or maybe you feel like your life is already so full and demanding that you barely have time to pray for the things right in front of you, let alone for people and places you do not know. Or you may be someone who already knows the joy of praying for strangers and others in foreign lands. Whatever your experience and position is, I pray that by the end of this chapter you will gain some new insights and sense your spiritual connection to the "friends you just haven't met yet" in our world.

One wants to finish life well. Paul said, "I have fought the good fight, I have finished the race, I have kept the faith..." (2 Timothy 4:7). The New Testament reveals Paul as one who dedicated his life to knowing God, being His servant, and doing His will. It was Jesus who came to Paul, revealing the Father's heart of love for him and initiating eternal purposes for his life. Is it really any different with us? God draws us to Himself with cords of love (Hosea 11:4), then provides opportunities for us to get acquainted with Him and, through His molding and shaping, develops us more and more into His likeness. It is vital for us to have His heart, for without it we will lack His love and have little real desire or passion to pray for and minister to people near and far to whom He may want to lead us. It is His plan to partner with us, as He did with Paul, in releasing His plans and purposes into the world.

Changing Hearts is God's Business

God longs for us to grow a heart like His. Like *His*? How can one portray the immensity of God - His power, wisdom, resources - let alone understand and grow a heart like His? Many people in God's world misunderstand His heart. In light of His Almightiness and the sheer size of His universe, many across the globe think He doesn't notice every speck of humanity He's created. "Does God know my name?" they wonder. "Does He really have a personal interest in me?" "Would He care about engaging His heart with mine?" Such questions can serve to create a hunger to increase our knowledge of God's heart. 1 John 4:8 tells us that "God is love." His tender, caring heart is revealed in Isaiah 40:28-29 which assures us that He never forgets us or is ignorant of our condition or needs. He is never too weak to act on our behalf; neither does He grow too weary to bless us with His strength in our trials. Even in judgment, His loving-kindness is present because "His compassions fail not" (Lamentations 3:22). Such is His love. Such is His heart!

If we are ever to participate in God's heavenly, loving economy at work in this earthly realm, we will need to grow a heart like His. You are likely thinking this won't be so easy. Right! But the good news is that God, who is always with us, stands ready to shape and mold us into His likeness. It is not an overnight process nor an easy one and most of us will need some heart surgery along the way... But growing a heart like God's is well worth the time and effort, for in the process we will gain many revelations of His character and ways and come to understand how greatly He cares about His world and the lives of the humanity He created.

The Bible has no shortage of lessons to teach us about transformation of the heart. There are many passages that speak of a "stony" heart in need of replacement with God's kind of heart. In the 36th chapter of Ezekiel, God is promising to renew His people after judgment for their idolatries. These words are part of His vow of restoration: *"I will give you a new heart and put a new spirit within you; I will take the heart of stone out of your flesh and give you a new heart of flesh"* (Ezekiel 36:26). Israel's "stony heart" was stubborn and self-willed; her promised "heart of flesh" would be pliable and responsive to God's will.

As a young believer, I was definitely aware of my own stony heart and regularly meditated on verses about this condition while asking the Lord to replace my heart of stone with His heart of flesh. In faithfulness, He began the work. Through the years I have often needed to return to these Scriptures and pray the same prayer whenever God would shine His searchlight into yet another area of my life that needed cleansing and renewal. Thankfully, growing God's heart is quite do-able because He is actually the one that brings the transformation to the willing heart. Our part is to admit our need, ask for His help, and submit to His leadings.

When it comes to the needs of others, do you sometimes notice resistance on your part in responding to them? Is there, quite possibly, a little hardness of heart? It is hard to admit when we are guilty of this. In our affluent American society, it's easy to become immune to the needs of people at home or far away. One day the Lord pointed this out to me when I drove by yet another homeless person seeking a handout. The incident happened quickly, and I wouldn't have thought more about it - except for a check from the Holy Spirit. Interestingly, He didn't call my attention to the needy person; it was my attitude He focused on. "I didn't ask you to size up that person's situation," my spiritual ears perceived. Embarrassed, my first response was defensive. My excuses wanted a chance to be heard: "Lord, I'm in a vulnerable position here being a woman alone with a child - it's not safe!" Quickly I heard more of my justifications as if a tape recorder was in playback mode: "If I give them money, it will go for alcohol or drugs... if they really need help, there are plenty of places in our community to serve them." Again I heard, "Why are you sizing up this situation, Ginny? I didn't call you to be a social worker; I called you to care about the people and things *I* care deeply about."

That day I went home and began to search the Scriptures for what

God has to say about the poor and needy. I was amazed at the discovery of His thoughts, intentions, plans for correction and blessing, and His first person examples for us to follow. "You shall open your hand wide to your brother, to your poor and needy, in your land," He instructs in Deuteronomy 15:11. And this Word that pierced my heart: "But he who honors Him (the Lord) has mercy on the needy" (Proverbs 14:31b).

My heart was being transformed by His Word. And after a time of self-examination under the Potter's eye, I began to better understand His heart in this area. I was crushed and truly sorry for my hardened attitude that had, over time, evolved into indifference. In thinking about it, I realized that I was unaware of when and where such thoughts had first entered my mind or even how long they had been in residence. But one thing I undoubtedly knew was that I wanted that way of thinking completely gone and replaced with God's heart (Ezekiel 36:26).

Walking in the Opposite Spirit

Often a lesson learned requires more than just our mental assent for the change to be lasting. Paul gives us a great teaching on this in an often overlooked passage from Ephesians 4:28 where he talks about a thief learning to successfully change his ways by what I call "walking in the opposite spirit." This expression simply means to act or behave in a way that is the opposite of the action and behavior that one wants to change. Putting this into practice when we become aware of an area of hardness in our thoughts and attitudes is one tangible way to aid us in growing a heart like God's.

Think this through with me for a moment. If a bank robber were between heists, would that mean that during the interim period he was no longer a thief? Not necessarily. In fact, even if years have gone by since his last robbery, one can't be certain that he/she is a changed person simply by the fact that it has been a long time since that person robbed a bank. Something will need to happen that produces a change on the inside; otherwise, the thief will always be at risk for stealing again. So what can the thief do to change his ways? Paul gives us the steps for changing entrenched behaviors. He begins by showing that it is not enough to simply stop the behavior. If there is to be genuine transformation, one must practice walking in the opposite spirit. He says "He who has been stealing must steal no longer, but must work, doing something useful with his own hands, that he may have something to share with those in need" (Ephesians 4:28). The following are Paul's specific steps for "walking in the opposite spirit" in the area of stealing:

- Stop the stealing (cease the wrong behavior or attitude)
- Go to work (earn an honest living; learn the lessons of submission)
- Do something useful with your hands (the very hands that once stole)
- Give to those in need (giving in place of perpetually taking)

After my encounter with the homeless person, the Father asked me to do something that would take me directly into the path of "walking in the opposite spirit." His request was perhaps a little out of the ordinary, but it would nonetheless be an answer to my prayer for God's heart to replace my heart of stone. Going forward, He prompted me to give twenty dollars to every person I encountered who was seeking a handout from me. Though being a single parent often meant financial struggle, I obediently did what He asked and began carrying with me twenty dollar bills to give out wherever I could safely do so. My son was young at the time, and I chuckle now remembering that after a season of observing this, he began urging me to give *more* than twenty dollars at each opportunity. Apparently he was perceiving an unlimited bank account! From this experience that lasted two years, I began to see and feel God's love for people in need in a new way. A life-changing, inside-out work was taking place in me. Indeed, He had begun to grow in me a heart like His own.

God's Economy of Giving

Have you ever noticed that God's economy, His management of resources, is often very different from our own? This fact is reflected in His own words, "For My thoughts are not your thoughts, nor are your ways My ways... For as the heavens are higher than the earth, so are My ways higher than your ways, and My thoughts than your thoughts" (Isaiah 55:8-9). Take, for example, God's *economy of giv-*

ing. He frequently moves in the heart of one person to give to another. In some cases it may involve sacrificial giving. Many times I have witnessed and even experienced first-hand this giving by one person to another only to see God meet the giver's need in an unexpected way at just the needed time. God knows all things, is in all things, and owns the cattle on a thousand hills (Psalm 50:10; Psalm 139). He distributes and redistributes His resources across the world, according to His economy of giving, often by using His people. This is yet another tangible reflection of His heart.

Thus, in God's economy of giving, He seeks people through whom He can bless others. The gift He may be asking you to give isn't always the tax-deductible kind or one for which the giver will be rewarded on earth. Nor does He require gifts of great size. Remember the five loaves and two fish offered by a lad amid the hungry crowd of five thousand? The disciple Andrew asked Jesus, "What are these among so many?" Yet the little lunch given into the hands of Jesus became a huge blessing. Even small measures of giving can accomplish great things! God's plans and ways, as said earlier, are higher and unlike our own. It isn't so much the amount or what kind of gift that pleases God; He focuses on the expression of the heart more than the outward sacrifice. And so He is in the process of molding us into useable vessels that reflect His heart. As He says in Jeremiah 18:6, "...like clay in the hand of the potter, so are you in My hand."

In a personal time of deep questioning one year, The Lord spoke to me from Isaiah 45:9, reminding me that He was the Potter and I was the clay. His message to me brought me back to a place of full dependence upon Him and the realization that I had been *squirming* under the Potter's hand and contending with his wisdom and ways as it pertains to His economy. Maybe, as you read this, you recognize yourself questioning or squirming under the Potter's hand. Our Lord sees our life from beginning to end, and just like the clay, we all become misshapen. But if we yield to the Potter's hand in all His ways, He will form us into a good vessel. One thing I know is that He is not looking for perfect people, just vessels willing to be molded and used for His purposes. Jesus Himself modeled this kind of submission when He yielded His will in the Garden of Gethsemane (Luke 22:42).

Mother Teresa - A Giver in God's Economy

There is probably no better example of a person who understood and lived out God's *economy of giving* than Mother Teresa. What could possibly possess a person like Mother Teresa, who came from Macedonia and a family of means earlier in her life, to leave the comfort of her own surroundings and to serve the poorest of the poor in Calcutta, India?

My friend, Anthony Gonzales, had the privilege of getting to know Mother Teresa in a friendship that blossomed over many years. It began while Anthony was in a seminary in Rome studying to become a Catholic priest and continued through the remaining years of Mother Teresa's life. Whenever she traveled to the San Francisco Bay area, where Anthony settled, she would request that he meet with her, and so he was blessed many times by these one-on-one visits. A number of friends and I have been the beneficiaries of some vibrantly rich stories surrounding Mother Teresa's life. On one occasion Anthony shared with us the story of her call by God that took place in 1948 in India. Jesus had revealed to her His plan for her to serve Him by ministering to some of the very poorest in His world. She was teaching in a Catholic school at the time and began pleading with her superiors to allow her to leave the school and go into the filthy streets of Calcutta. Though not knowing exactly what she would be doing or how she would accomplish it, Mother Teresa was sure of God's leading and knew that she must follow His call. Without any solid plan, and being frail in nature, her request was met with resistance for nearly a year. Finally her superiors relented and the Lord brought added confirmation that it was time when a couple provided a room for her in which to live.

One day Mother was going to teach the street children in Calcutta when she heard a groaning noise coming from one of the back alleyways. She followed the sound to discover an old woman in a trashcan half eaten by rats and ants and covered with maggots. All the desperate woman could manage to say was, "My son threw me away. My son threw me away." Mother Teresa, in her slight 4'10" frame, literally picked her up and carried her to the nearest hospital for treatment. Sadly, all help for the desperate woman was refused. The hospital workers insisted that they could not accommodate such people since the streets were filled with them. If they took in some, help for all would be expected. Mother Teresa persisted and refused to leave, insisting that, at the very least, she be given some clean rags and water to wash the woman's wounds.. This was allowed, and she did her best, finally holding the poor woman in her arms until she died.

Watching the old woman in her arms taking her final breaths, Mother Teresa heard the Lord tell her that He comes in *distressing disguises*. From then on, she knew that she would always serve the world's very poorest – this was to be her life's mission. The launch of her ministry was in God's perfect timing as many of her students from the school where she had taught became the first Sisters to join her order, the Missionaries of Charity. This order, which would eventually be established world-wide, today has over 4500 Sisters and nearly 550 Missions.

Mother Teresa gave her life to serve Jesus in His *distressing disguise* as the poorest of the poor. She did not receive anything materially from those she served. In fact, she refused any material thing for herself, choosing to live at the same level of poverty as those she helped. Rather than benefiting from the riches of the world, Mother Teresa benefited from God's *economy of giving*, for she was the recipient of His richest blessings and promises. She was a woman whose heart reflected God's and who understood the power of prayer to affect her little corner of the world. In her own words, "Prayer enlarges the heart until it is capable of containing God's gift of Himself." She knew the joy of answered prayer, spiritual rewards, and treasure in Heaven (Isaiah 58:9; Proverbs 14:21; Proverbs 19:17; Matthew 25:31-46; Luke 12:33-34).

Mother Teresa exemplifies what it means to be a useable vessel in the hand of the Potter, a woman beautifully drawn in to God's rich *economy of giving*. Ultimately her life, her prayers, her heart and ministry affected people and nations worldwide

God's Economy of Prayer
Not many of us will personally identify with the mission call that

Mother Teresa had on her life, although we certainly have a high regard for her sacrificial and prayerful work. Reflecting on her life of ministry, who could say where her prayers began and where they ended as each day they appeared to play themselves out in Divine orchestration. Though we may not be called to mission work, we can always be present in prayer. There is no limit to where one can go in prayer, quite literally travelling the world unseen and unknown.

It took a while in my Christian life for me to figure out that God is also an initiator of prayer. As a young believer I thought that prayer was all about those things we did for Him. A time came when I was feeling a bit proud of myself because I was inviting Jesus into all my plans. One day He whispered to me, "Ginny, I am glad you bring me into everything in your life, but it would be even better if you would let Me bring you into Mine and for you to seek what is on my heart and mind." That revelation was another turning point in my spiritual journey. My awareness and interest began to increase dramatically for those things which concerned the Lord. I absolutely marveled (and still do) at the idea that God would want to share with me what is on His mind.

During one ten year period, I was keenly aware of the Lord prompting me to pray for Russia. At that time I felt certain that my prayers were being lifted up in unison with many others, forming a concert of prayer. Then came another period of time when the Lord called and energized me to pray for a particular couple in mission work. More recently, I can point to a day when I was lunching with my friend Gini, telling her how I had called a mutual friend for prayer about a certain matter. She thought and then said, "You called Marlene and God called me." Such is His *economy of prayer* at work leading us to pray what is on His heart – in the last case, doubling it!

If our spiritual ears are open, we can expect God to call us often to pray for many places, people, and situations. We may not always know the outcome or impact of our prayers, but as I have grown in my understanding of God's *economy of prayer* over the years, I have come to understand that every prayer counts. Though unseen they are never unheard. If you are not already engaged in this kind of exciting, energizing prayer activity that reaches people both near and far, you can be! One easy way to begin is by praying for your neighbors and watching God go to work. The following story illustrates one such rewarding effort of mine.

A neighbor of mine who was the matriarch of a large family had died, and I felt prompted to visit and offer prayer. Since I didn't really know the family, I asked my next door neighbor, who knew them well, to join me. Initially she was hesitant because the family was of a different faith expression. But later in the day, armed with plenty of food and goodwill, we went to the home. As we approached I noticed many people gathered both inside and outside, all with the same stoic faces and placid demeanor. The mood was somber and eerily quiet. The adult daughters greeted us in the kitchen and I quietly asked if we could pray for them. One of the women said, "Wait, I will be right back." She left the kitchen and returned in a few minutes. Without saying anything further, she motioned for us to follow her down the hallway to a bedroom. I assumed she was taking us to a private area where probably only a few family members were gathered. Imagine my shock when she led us into a room where her deceased mother was lying on the bed. It was now 5:00 pm and she had died at 5:00 that morning.

It would not be an exaggeration to say that I suddenly felt I was in over my head. As if to read my mind, my accompanying neighbor friend was looking at me as if to say, "So what are you going to do now, Watson?" My sentiments exactly! I shot up a quick prayer of one word: "Help!" Then slowly I extended my hands to either side and family members quickly grasped them, as well as one another's. In the quietness of the room where we stood holding hands, I began speaking the Lord's Prayer and soon heard a gentle hum of voices join in. What I didn't realize at the time was that a line of almost thirty people, hands joined, had begun to extend all the way down the hallway, through much of the house, and into the garage. As my neighbor and I left, the family members and friends were still clasping each other's hands. Their tear-streaked faces, now softened and relaxed, were smiling as they thanked us for coming.

In this family's tradition, the Priest is called to come before the deceased is removed from the home. The family had been holding vigil all day waiting for the Priest to release their dear departed mother into the hands of God. The family could do little but wait until that time came. In the interim, I became their Priest. I can only say how glad I am that I didn't know in advance what the Lord or the family needed from me, and I am *exceedingly* glad that He equipped me to do what was needed!

Was I scared? Yes! There would have been no anxiety had I not gotten involved at all. I had no idea what I was walking into, and no one had asked me to make the visit...that is, no one but the Lord Himself. I see this as another example of His *economy of prayer*. In a million years, would I ever have imagined that through this small act of obedience I would literally be leading thirty-plus people unknown to me in prayer via a human prayer chain? Absolutely not! But God knew and multiplied the resulting blessing far beyond anything I could have planned.

No one is a Stranger to God

God's *economy of giving* and *economy of prayer* are ways through which He seeks to balance the scales of justice in the world He so deeply loves. When people are moldable and pliable in the Potter's hands, they begin to carry out His plans for expressing love and justice in ways that far exceed any man-made plans.

Scripture teaches that "from one man he (God) made every nation of men, that they should inhabit the whole earth; and he determined the times set for them and the exact places where each of us would live" (Acts 17:26-28). Thus all people are of one family, each living in their appointed place. Whether that homeland is India or America or any other place on the earth, Jesus comes to all of us - as He did to Mother Teresa -in His *distressing disguises* to remind us that we all belong to one another and we are all people in need (Matthew 25:42-45).

Henry Blackaby, pastor and author of the acclaimed book, *Experiencing God,* is well known for his statement, "Find out where God is working and join Him." God's heart can clearly be seen in His activity worldwide that is drawing all men to one day live peaceably together under His Kingdom rule. We are assured of this happening since God has already prophesied the salvation of the nations (Isaiah 52:10) which now includes 24,000 people groups. Meanwhile, according to David Sitton, lifelong missionary and author of the book *Reckless Abandon*, 2.8 million people are still waiting to hear the gospel. How many praying people will it take?

If this is your first introduction to praying for the nations I have great news for you! Thankfully, our prayers are not the beginning point. God was and is and has always been since the beginning of time. We are not working with a blank slate as God has already set the stage and gone before us to establish Himself and His rule upon earth. The earth is no longer formless and void. His fingerprints are deeply embedded in all of creation which continually declares His glory and proclaims the works of His hands (Psalm 19:1). Scripture tells us that since the creation of the world, God's invisible qualities - His eternal power and divine nature - have been clearly seen, being understood from what has been made, so that men are without excuse (Romans 1:20). In other words, God has spoken enough through His creation for all men to know that He exists and that it is His handiwork they witness. Just as powerful as the Spirit of God who brooded over the dark, formless, empty earth just prior to creation, is God's Spirit today that continues to hover over the nations. Eventually "every knee will bow and every tongue confess that Jesus Christ is Lord" (Romans 14:11). When we pray we are in lockstep with God's plan for the world and are invited, as one who is a guest of honor with a front row seat, to His unfolding purpose. You can be assured that as you hover in prayer for people you do not know in countries unfamiliar to you, you have indeed found where God is working and have joined with Him in what He is already doing!

When my son Jordan was very young, he had a prayer partner in Honduras named Kenslee, the son of a pastor we had met. This prayer partnership came about as part of a Sunday School project where all the children adopted a child in Honduras for prayer. Jordan faithfully prayed for Kenslee every night for almost eight years. The initial prayers for his young prayer partner were very short and completely centered on Kenslee. But as time went by, I was amazed to hear his prayers grow in their magnitude until eventually he was praying not only for Kenslee but for the entire country of Honduras! I still remember it vividly today and can hear his tender, sweet voice praying, "And Lord, I want to pray for ALL the people in Honduras - even though they are not my praying partners." Hearing these simple but earnest prayers nightly over the years, I could literally feel a delight in God's heart. My own heart was sometimes so full while listening to my son that I thought it would burst with joy!

I'm convinced that as you seek to grow God's heart in prayer for the nations, you, too, will experience what happened to my son Jordan. You can begin by planting a seed with simple, short prayers for a stranger or another country. As you are faithful in praying, the Lord will enlarge your heart to include other things that are on His heart, just as He did with Jordan when he was praying for a little boy he had never met in a country far away.

Won't you join with me in becoming part of the *human prayer chain* around the globe where no one is a stranger to God (John 3:16)?

Do-Able Prayers for Growing God's Heart for the World

■ Ask God to reveal if you have a "stony" heart when it comes to praying for people and places you do not know (1 John 1:9).

■ Once God shows you an area of hardness, confess and ask His forgiveness. Then ask Him to replace it with His heart of love (Ezekiel 36:26).

■ Ask God to share with you what is on His heart and mind (Isaiah 55:8-9; Luke 2:49).

■ Pray that God will resurrect and protect the spiritual boundaries of the country in which you live and that He will become her rightful ruler (Acts 17:24-28).

■ Pray a "blessing" prayer for your family's country of origin. Remember the *Miracle in Sweden* story from chapter 7? I have a Swedish keychain attached to my Bible cover to keep my beloved Sweden in the forefront of my mind for prayer. Even if you are 100 or more years removed from your ancestors and their country of origin (as I was), there is still a connection in the spiritual realm uniting you with them and giving you a level of authority in prayer for that country (Proverbs 29:18; 2 Chronicles 7:14; Numbers 6:22-27).

■ Find some existing connection points with missionaries or countries that you or your church already have and use them as a starting point for prayer.

■ Pray for those in authority and in leadership (1 Timothy 2:1-4).

God said "Ask of me, and I will give the nations for your inheritance, the uttermost parts of the earth for your possession" (Psalm 2:8).

IN SUMMARY – Chapter 8

No one is a stranger to God. He knows and is profoundly interested in every person He has created. Through his *economy of giving* and *economy of prayer* He seeks to balance the scales of justice in the world. As each of us adds our prayers to the growing chorus of prayer around the world, we become part of the ever-expanding human prayer chain stepping in to God's hotbed of spiritual activity around the globe.

Key Verses: Acts 17:26-28; Matthew 25:42-45

STUDY/DISCUSSION/REFLECTION QUESTIONS

1. What does the Bible tell us about a stony heart (Ezekiel 11:19, 36:26; Jeremiah 24:7; Psalm 51:10)?

2. Do these verses speak only to those who are stiff-necked and obstinate? Elaborate.

3. Create a scenario where existing behavior needs to change. Then identify steps for "walking in the opposite spirit" to overcome that behavior. Refer back to this section in the chapter.

4. What does the term "God's economy for giving" mean? What might be an example?

5. What does the term "God's economy for praying" mean? What would be an example?

6. What are some similarities between #4 and #5?

7. What does it mean that no one is a stranger to God?

8. In what ways does this chapter encourage you to pray for the Nation(s)? How will you begin?

Use "*Do-Able Prayers* for Growing God's Heart for the World" as a guide for your prayer time.

DIG DEEPER - Optional; refer to suggestions page

These passages were referenced in this chapter: *Acts 17:26; 2 Timothy 4:7; Hosea 11:4; 1 John 4:8; Isaiah 40:28-29; Lamentations 3:22; Ezekiel 36:26; Deuteronomy 15:11; Proverbs 14:31b; Ephesians 4:28; Psalm 50:10; Psalm 139; Jeremiah 18:6; Isaiah 45:9; Luke 22:42; Isaiah 58:9; Proverbs 14:21; Proverbs 19:17; Matthew 25:31-46; Luke 12:33-34; Acts 17:26-28; Matthew 25:42-45; Isaiah 52:10; Psalm 19:1; Romans 1:20; Romans 14:11; John 3:16; 1 John 1:9; Ezekiel 36:26; Isaiah 55:8-9; Luke 2:49; Acts 17:24-28; Proverbs 29:18; 2 Chronicles 7:14; Numbers 6:22-27; 1 Timothy 2:1-4; Psalm 2:8*

A Note From the Author

Congratulations and thank you for finishing eight chapters of a book I have loved writing. For me, the writing was a form of prayer I took in and breathed out during the process. Most of us are acquainted with the catch phrase, "It takes a village to raise a child." My "village" of friends, prayer partners, and co-laborers in Christ has supported me with love and helping hands to raise up this book and also to pray for each of you who reads it.

I've often been reminded that my life is a dress rehearsal, performed before an *audience of One,* for my time in eternity. My heartfelt prayer is that the prayer encouragements in the pages of this book have drawn you closer to the *One* and will affect your life that is passing before His view. If *Do-Able Prayer* has spoken to you in a particular way or encouraged you in a special way, I would love to hear from you! (Contact information is at the end of this note as well as on the inside cover).

In Dennis Linn's acclaimed *Sleeping with Bread,* an account is given of thousands of orphaned, homeless children left to starve after the bombing raids of World War II. Some were rescued and placed in refugee camps where they were cared for and no longer needed to worry about food and shelter. Even so, because of the great losses many of these children had suffered, they could not sleep at night. Many were afraid of waking up and finding themselves once again without a home or food. Nothing seemed to relieve their anxiety. Finally someone came up with the idea of giving each child a piece of bread to hold onto at bedtime. This plan quickly worked wonders in returning the children to peaceful sleep.

Prayer, to God's children, is as bread was to these orphans. In one very definite way we can relate to how those children felt, for at the core of our being we can never feel fully secure and at home as long as earth is our dwelling place. The Bible tells us that we are so-journers in a foreign land (Leviticus 25:23). Our earthly bodies and spirits are always longing for their eternal home. We, too, need something to hold onto. When prayer becomes a way of life for us, it brings us into that place of peace and security in much the same way the bedtime bread dispelled the orphan children's anxiety and brought a peaceful inner calm. One web blogger says, "We need bread - bread to eat and bread to give away, bread to sleep and bread to carry us on the journey..."

Prayer is a form of bread we give away. Paul urges us in 1 Timothy 2:1-2 to pray for everyone: "I urge, then, first of all, that requests, prayers, intercessions and thanksgiving be made for everyone - for kings and all those in authority." And then he tells why: "...that we may live peaceful and quiet lives in all godliness and holiness." Paul continues on, telling believers how God feels about this kind of pray-ing: "For this is good, and pleases God our Savior, who wants all men to be saved and to come to a knowledge of the truth."

How different might our families, cities, nations, and the world be if we each become God's useable vessel dispensing prayer wherever we go. For people living in homes where violence exists or in war torn countries, the idea of living a peaceful and quiet life may seem like an impossible dream. Yet, while that violent home may have no one to stand guard for it, a watchful Christian neighbor could stand in the gap and cover it in prayer. These are critical times when believers need to be on "high alert" in the spiritual realm. The need for builders of the *Prayer Wall* is uppermost in God's heart in light of the mount-ing evil and afflictions of life and the evidence of oncoming judgment.

Regardless of the length or breadth of our prayers, they have the power to actually change destiny in human affairs. In the area where I live, signs dot the freeways naming various groups and companies who have adopted specific areas along the roadway which they vol-untarily "clean up." When Christians pray for their sphere of influ-ence, they are like these groups who clean up particular stretches of the highway. The difference is that they are performing "spiritual clean-up" works. It is as if they are scraping the filth of the earth into sanitizing buckets for God's glory! Prayer by prayer we invite the Holy Spirit to remove the litter deployed by the enemy and restore what has been ravaged.

John Robb, Chairman for the International Prayer Council, expresses it this way "It could be said that the future of our planet is now in the hands and hearts of today's intercessors." I would expand that to say "in the hands and hearts of *all* the people who pray." He continues on to say "These are people who share God's heart, allowing His Word and Spirit to guide their praying as they encounter the world in all its disturbing darkness and hopeful possibility. Having more access to late-breaking and comprehensive information than any other generation before us, we have an unprecedented and awesome privilege to shape history through prayer."

In this book it has been my aim to inspire you to grow into a praying lifestyle in which you pray often into the traffic of life, finding your place on the *Wall of Prayer,* as one who will become part of shaping history through prayer. Together we will find joy as we discover the multi-faceted art of prayer that networks us together across the world. Keep prayer close to you just as the orphan children kept their bread close to them during the night.

Spiritual advancements are usually accompanied by enemy threats. Our battle, according to Ephesians 6:12, is not an earthly one. We wrestle against "principalities, against powers, against the rulers of the darkness of this age, against spiritual hosts of wickedness in the heavenly places..." We can count on Satan to be right behind any Kingdom efforts with his derailing strategies (1 Peter 5:8). We need not be fearful but alert to the enemy's tactics to bring discouragement and doubts into our minds as we take steps forward in our prayer life. In his book *The Invisible War,* Chip Ingram simplifies it for us: "There are reasons that prayer doesn't always come easily for us; we have enemies who want to make it difficult."

In Zechariah's account of the thousands of Jews returning to Jerusalem after seventy years of exile in Babylon, we read that they found the walls of their city broken down and the temple completely destroyed. As workers began rebuilding the temple, many efforts were made to hinder them. Their enemies were snipers who took advantage of the fact that they had no city wall to protect them. Thus came the Lord's word to the prophet Zechariah telling Jerusalem, "I will be a wall of fire all around her, and I will be the glory in her midst" (Zechariah 2:5). What a reassuring promise! The temple was rebuilt because the Lord encircled His people, becoming their *Wall of Fire*. Is there any security so certain as that based on God's promise, not only of His protection but of His blessed presence - "the glory in her midst?"

We can be assured that as we take up our "armor" (weapons of warfare - Ephesians 6) and stand firm against the adversary's attacks, God will be our protector. When we assertively speak, "Get thee behind me, Satan" and continue being about the Lord's business, God Himself will encircle us with His Holy Spirit *Wall of Fire* (Acts 10:38; Matthew 16:23; John 14:31). Indeed, "He who began a good work in you *will* bring it to completion" (Philippians 1:6).

I pray that reading *Do-Able Prayer* has inspired you to pray in the intersections of your life. I pray that you will long to hear harsh words met with a "gentle answer that turns away wrath" (Proverbs 15:1). May you declare in prayer for another that God will watch over them in their coming and going (Psalm 121:8). I pray that you will want to pray God's promises of goodness, graciousness and compassion over your family and others, and that you will routinely pray blessings when you leave a home that is worthy (1 Samuel 25:6; Matthew 10:13). I pray that you will grow a heart like God's and be filled with His mercy and compassion for the world He so dearly loves!

Now may...

"The LORD bless you and keep you; the LORD make his face shine on you and be gracious to you; the LORD turn his face toward you and give you peace" (Numbers 6:24-26).

With the affectionate love of Christ our Savior,

Ginny Kisling
ginny@harvestprayer.com
gkisling@pacbell.net

I owe it all to Him.

Prayer Glossary

Armor of God – Spiritual armor worn by believers to ward off Satan's fiery darts (See Ephesians 6:13-18. Examples include the belt of truth and shield of faith given by the Lord).

Do-Able Prayer – Prayer that can easily be done in the traffic and intersections of life

Field of Service – A specific area of duty or service that God gives to every Christian

Five Percenters – Those (including Intercessors, Prayer Warriors and Watchmen) who have a natural passion to pray

Intercessors: Those who are often called to represent others or specific situations and needs before God (Though every believer is called to pray, Intercessors have a special passion to do so).

Ninety-five Percenters – Those Christians who are distinct from the Five Percenters but are growing in their prayer life

Passionate-in-prayer –Describes individuals who have a special fervor or zeal to pray

Prayer Assignment – An appointment by God to pray for a specific purpose

Prayer Ministry – A recognized area of ministry by a local church body

Prayer Warrior - One who battles in prayer the powers of darkness in the spiritual realm to enforce Christ's victory at the Cross (people who often are unwilling to "let go" until released by the Lord from an assignment of long or short duration)

Spiritual Homesteading – Gaining, retaining, and building a position of authority in spiritual territory given by the Lord to a believer for His Kingdom purposes

Stronghold– An entrenched mindset or system of false thinking or beliefs used as arguments against God and to keep men from finding Him

Throne Room of God –Place of God's presence and rule to which believers come in prayer

Voice of Prayer –The voice lifted to God in praise, worship, thanksgiving and petition

Wall of Prayer – Prayer whose extent or "volume" is critical in serving to protect homes, churches, cities and nations

Watchmen: Alert, watchful people of prayer who generally carry broader assignments from the Lord , especially involving prayer for the protection of church leaders, the Church at large, and for territories, cities, and the nations

End Notes

Chapter One: The Five Percenters

■ C. Peter Wagner, *Prayer Shield* (Ontario, CA: Regal Books 1992)

■ Mount Athos-20 Monastaries:
http://www.youtube.com/watch?v=A0OkDLyLamU (60 minute Interview)
http://www.inathos.gr/athos/en/ - Main Website
http://www.mountathos.co.uk/ - The journey of 3 Englishmen to Mount Athos

Chapter Two: The Ninety-five Percenters

■ Norman Percy Grubb, *Rees Howells, Intercessor* (Britain, British Publishers, 1952)

■ Doris M. Ruscoe, *The Intercession of Rees Howells* (Britain, The Lutterworth Press, 1983)

■ http://www.biblecollegeofwales.org/

■ Jonathan Graf, *Praying Like Paul* (Indiana, Prayer Shop Publishing 2008)

■ David and Kim Butts, *Pray Like the King* (Indiana, Prayer Shop Publishing, 2007)

■ Max Lucado, *He Still Moves Stones* (Nashville, Tennessee, Word Publishing Group, 1993), 92.

Chapter Four: Protect and Sanctify Your Home

■ Chip Ingram, *The Invisible War* (Grand Rapids, Michigan: Baker Books, 2006)

■ Frances Goodrich, Albert Hackett, Frank Capa, Joe Swerling, Phillip Van Doren Stern, *It's a Wonderful Life* (1946)

■ Thomas Kinkade, *Thomas Kinkade Gallery* (www.thomaskinkade.com)

Chapter Five: Turning Your Thoughts Into Prayers
■ Crabb, Larry, *Connecting: healing ourselves and our relationships* (Nashville, Tennessee: W Publishing Group, 2005), 47.

Chapter Six: Fortifying the Wall of Prayer in Your Church
■ Kinnaman, David, *You Lost Me* (Grand Rapid, Michigan: Baker Books, 2011)
■ CNN Reports, 9/27/2011
■ www.focusonthefamily.com

Chapter Eight: God's Heart for the Nations
■ David Sitton, *Reckless Abandon* (Ambassador International 2011)
■ Henry Blackaby, *Experiencing God* (Nashville, Tennesee: B&H Books, 2008)

Note from the Author
■ Dennis Linn, *Sleeping with Bread* (Mahwah, New Jersey: Paulist Press, 1995), 1
■ Chip Ingrahm, *The Invisible War* (Grand Rapid, Michigan: Baker Books, 2006)

Featured Prayer Resources

Faith Alive Christian Resources:
www.faithaliversources.org

DEVOTIONALS
Twilight **by Andrew Kuyvenhoven**
This newly updated companion to the bestselling devotional
Daylight leads you through an entire year of meaningful moments
with God.
Seeking God's Face **by Philip F. Reinders**
An entire year of daily prayers and readings based on the
ancient practice of the "Daily Office"

WWW.PRAYERSHOP.ORG – The world's largest only prayer
Webstore with over 600 resources – www.prayershop.org

PRAYER ENCOURAGERS
The Power of Personal Prayer **by Jonathan Graf**
*One of the easiest to read and understand treatments of prayer on
the market today*

Outside the Camp **by Terry Teykl**
A thirty-day prayer guide that teaches you to inquire of the Lord

Love to Pray **by Alvin VanderGriend** (also available in Spanish)
A 40-day devotional that will transform your prayer life

The Practice of the Presence of God **by Brother Lawrence**
*Brother Lawrence, a man of humble beginnings, models for us the
art of practicing the presence of God.*

Pray Like the King **by David & Kim Butts**
Lessons from the Prayers of Israel's Kings

Prayer Shield by Dr. C. Peter Wagner
How to Intercede for Pastors, Christian Leaders, and Others on the Spiritual Frontlines
Praying God's Word Day by Day by Beth Moore
Ever feel tongue-tied while talking with God? Discover the joys of praying Scripture and you'll boldly approach God's throne with the very mind and words of Christ!

FAMILY
The Praying Family by Kim Butts
The Praying Family is for those who desire a consistent and powerful prayer life for their families.
KidsGap: Teaching Children To Be Kingdom Intercessors by Jenny Almquist
These twelve action-packed lessons on prayer will help your children to become powerful kingdom intercessors.
Prayer Saturated Kids: by Arlyn Lawrence and Cheryl Sacks
Empowering and Equipping Children in Prayer

FOR THE CHURCH
Fresh Encounters by Daniel Henderson
Learn about the power of praying together
Asleep in the Land of Nod by David Butts
Thirty Days Toward Awakening the Church

LEADERS
The Prayer Saturated Church: A Comprehensive Handbook for Leaders by Cheryl Sacks *This landmark book provides all the step-by-step, practical help a pastor or prayer leader needs to mobilize, organize, and motivate believers to make their church a house of prayer.*

About the Author

Ginny is a self-supporting missionary who makes her home in Northern California along with her son Jordan.

Working in the prayer ministry since 1996, Ginny is a teacher and mentor to many. In addition to working within her church, she has mobilized and given prayer leadership to many Bay Area campaigns including Dr. Billy Graham Crusade, three Promise Keeper events, Harvest Crusade and served as a county leader for a 10 county-wide prayer initiative known as "Canopy of Prayer" that culminated with intensive prayer coverage by land, sea and air.

Ginny works for Harvest Prayer Ministries, a national prayer organization out of Terre Haute, Indiana, that is dedicated to helping churches become "Houses of Prayer." As the Western Regional Director for CPLN (a part of Harvest Prayer Ministries) she has orchestrated and led multiple Bay Area regional equipping prayer conferences.

As a passionate speaker and consultant, Ginny is eager to see prayer activated among all of God's people, not just the passionate few. If you are ready to see prayer ignited in your group or church, please contact Ginny to discuss speaking opportunities and the needs of your group.

If you would be interested in joining Ginny's prayer and ministry support team, you can reach her at the below contact information.

Ginny Kisling
Ask Ginny about her *Signature Do-Able Prayer Events*
ginny@harvestprayer.com
gkisling@pacbell.net

Made in the USA
Charleston, SC
18 June 2012